IELTS

SUCCESS

IN

ESSAY

WRITING

AMRITASHAAN

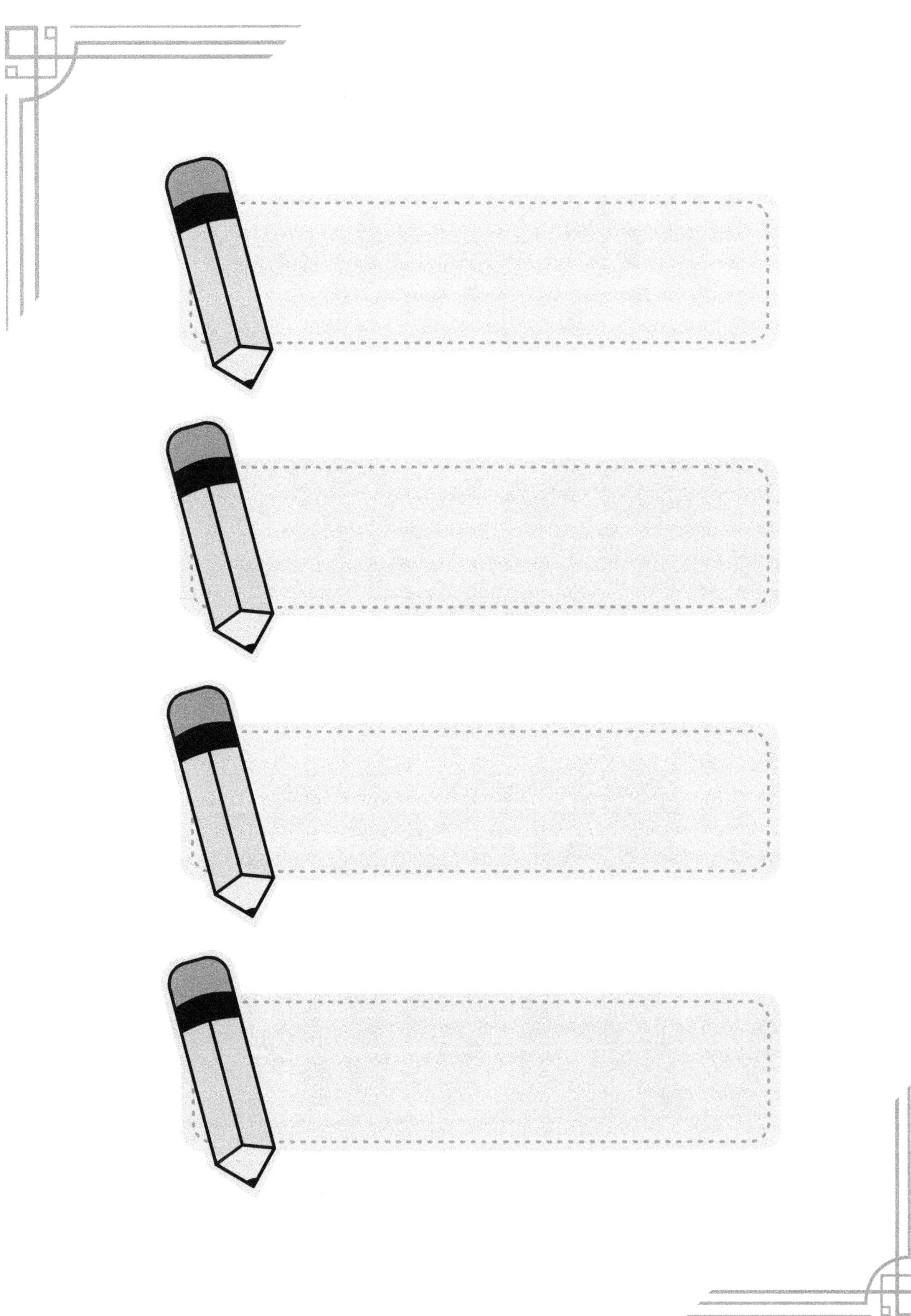

GENERAL & ACADEMIC ESSAYS

100+ MODEL ANSWERS

PREPARE FOR HIGH BANDS

Published : October, 2023.

AMRITASHAAN

TABLE OF CONTENTS

TABLE OF CONTENTS

TABLE OF CONTENTS

TABLE OF CONTENTS

TO WHAT EXTENT DO AGREE

TABLE OF CONTENTS

TABLE OF CONTENTS

IELTS Success in Essay Writing | Amritashaan

TABLE OF CONTENTS

REASONS - POSITIVE OR NEGATIVE CHANGE

MISCELLANEOUS TOPICS

TABLE OF CONTENTS

TABLE OF CONTENTS

ADD WORDS TO YOUR VOCABULARY

TABLE OF CONTENTS

LEARN TO WRITE A RANGE OF SENTENCES

WELCOME MESSAGE

Dear Reader,

Greetings!

It is good to see that you have picked the book out of many books on the book rack. A desire for great success makes us hunt for good books. Your time is important and i am very sure the book will prove a big help in realizing your dreams.

The book of IELTS essays has been composed for aspirants like you who have high aims in life to achieve. The contents of the book have been arranged in such a way that the book will not only take your essay writing skill to next level but it would also give you insight to ponder over situations.

I firmly believe the book 'IELTS Success in Essay Writing' will make your journey of IELTS Writing Essay easy, you will be able to understand the technique of effective writing, prepare well and importantly you will appreciate your choice of picking up the book.

Wishing you Happy reading & High Bands!

Amritashaan

A Humble Dedication

To my father, the one who instilled in me the
importance of self-contentment,
To my mom, the one who showed me the value of
perseverance without seeking recognition;
To my brother, forever grateful for his constant
support and admiration,
To my loving sister, who has an unparalleled love for
me;
To my caring sister-in-law, a true source of
support and care in my life,
To my uncle, the epitome of passion and dedication
in his work, forever inspiring me!

Our appreciation goes out to Manav Khanna, for his
invaluable contribution as the editor of this book.

AMRITASHAAN
Author

About Me

AMRITASHAAN is a dynamic educator and with a post graduate degree in English literature, an IELTS & PTE institute AMUSE CONSULTANTS owner, a certified trainer has dedicated her career to explore new methods of teaching and training individuals to achieve fluency in Speaking and writing English.

Professional Experience

In the beginning of her career, she groomed hundreds of local kids from ICSE, CBSE and state boards in grammar and tailored many practice lessons and practice papers to guide them with the radicals of the language. For over decade she conducted classes for the students of graduation and post graduation guiding them in English literature and facilitated the learners achieve their dream of becoming English teacher or getting dream jobs with their language skills. For over a couple of decades, Amrita taught IELTS and English as a foreign language to both native Indians and non-native speakers in India. Her interactive teaching style and student-centered approach helped many of her students excel in their language proficiency exams.

Achievements

In 2020, Amrita decided to follow her passion for writing during the lockdown time of Covid Pandemic. Her debut book, **"EMBELLISH YOUR ENGLISH"** is a collection of small and interesting chapters which takes the the readers to next level of English by enhancing their word power. The book not only makes your English beautiful but generates your interest in reading good English books. She has always been a source of inspiration for her learners. Her personally designed English learning software **AMUSE – Amrita Makes You Speak English,** a website www.easybreezyenglish4u.com and Youtube channel EASY BREEZY ENGLISH 4U are other reputed assets helping the English learners.

PREFACE

This book is meant to help not only an average student crack the IELTS essay but also to guide a good learner how to score high bands in writing essay. Over the years, I have seen fairly good students struggling with writing essay, they failed in getting desired result.

Though teaching itself is more than a learning session for a trainer but formal sessions with expert guides of British Council and IDP during Train The Trainer programs was wonderful time for accumulating knowledge of formal structure of IELTS writing modules.

By guiding and grooming thousands of students for their writing skills, I have checked their writings almost every day and thus have a clear view where students lack and where they go out of track while writing in exam. The IELTS essay has to have a plan. Time spent on the plan, is time well invested.

A planned essay helps students produce a well structured essay with relevant reasons. A crisp, but brief and to-the-point introduction and conclusion, and two to three well planned paragraphs with logic reasons, is all that is required for the IELTS essays.

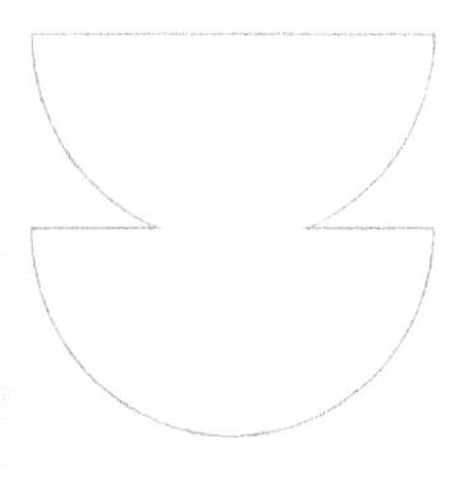

IELTS ESSAY WRITING

Effective essay writing allows individuals to express themselves clearly and convincingly – a valuable skill in many fields. The book is a handy tool for anyone preparing to take the IELTS exam. It not only helps individuals to develop their writing skills but also provides a thorough understanding of the exam format and requirements.

Writing an effective essay requires critical thinking, organized presentation of ideas and good language proficiency. The book helps to learn these essential skills to succeed on the IELTS exam besides proficient essay writing abilities prove advantageous in both academic and professional contexts beyond the exam setting. By and large, the book intends to help you develop essay-writing abilities for tackling the IELTS exam successfully as well as bolstering your writing acumen in general.

Some people believe that people who read books can develop more imagination and language skills than those who prefer to watch TV. Do you agree or disagree?

People persistently endeavor to refine their creative skills and language aptitude by utilizing various means. It is generally observed that these skills can better be enhanced by reading books than by watching shows on television. I would like to stand strongly in accord with the statement as book reading is a conducive activity in comparison of watching television for the skills mentioned.

My perception makes me believe that books are the greatest source of knowledge and information where the words carry the power to create pictorial world in a reader's mind. The stories transport the readers into the world of imagination and they see the things happening on the screen of their mind. Reading works as a catalyst which ignites the power of fantasizing. For example, a child while reading some chapter of history visualizes the event and thus goes imaginative.

To add on, books are read with the mindset to enhance linguistic skills. The more one reads, the more he comprehends the radicals of the language. The words, phrases, collocations used in articles add to the word power of the readers.

Alternatively, television is a small box of entertainment basically which is accessed to spend some leisure hours. Although there are many knowledgeable and informative programs which may help polishing different skills but viewers hardly switch on the screen with the intention to learn something. To make it more clear, for working on grammar or vocabulary, one will get some book of the same genre and read it instead of watching a live cricket match in some sports channel.

Most importantly, television being a source of recreation, can be taken as a way to distraction rather than a means of stimulating creativity. People who watch too much television often find themselves in a state of mind-numbing repetition which can erode creative thinking skills and decrease motivation eventually leading to the distraction from pursuing creative endeavors such as painting, writing, or playing music.

To wrap up, it is rightly assumed by people that book reading is more helpful in improving mental agility and linguistic skills as books not only create pictorial world but are also written with the same objective. Expecting same benefits from TV watching which is a box of entertainment basically would not be very fair.

Some teachers think international student exchange would be beneficial for all teenage school students. Do you think its advantages outweigh the disadvantages?

International student exchange program is a practice that is adopted by some educational institutions in which the learner are sent to overseas colleges and universities for a short period of time. Realizing the significance of such programs some educators firmly perceive that if such programs are organized, it will be highly beneficial for the learners. Before drawing any conclusion, I need to weigh both the sides.

Counting the benedictions, when students join such a program, they feel extremely excited that they are getting a great opportunity of learning an international program. The enthusiasm exhibits how curious they are to amass knowledge from universities abroad.

To add on, studying in an international institute give them exposure of the culture and language of the country they are in. They get to know that there exists another world outside their books. Knowledge, experience and confidence they accumulate make them more analytical in their thinking. For example, international programs make them learn practical skills where they learn how to put the knowledge into practice. Importantly, the diverse skills and experiences gained from these programs make students more attractive to employers and open up doors to global career opportunities.

Alternatively, there are some demerits of these programs too. Firstly going abroad is not an easily affordable affair for the pupils coming from under privileged section of society who cannot afford the high expenditure.

Then, inspite of best arrangements, living in a foreign country, can be incredibly isolating leading to feelings of homesickness, anxiety and depression.

Counting next, after experiencing a foreign culture and language, students may struggle to readjust to their own academic environments and instead of reaping benefit, may end up in poor academic performance.

After enumerating some pros and cons, I conclude that despite some drawbacks, its advantages overshadow because students get opportunity to visit international society and get exposure to new culture, language, novel methods and techniques of learning which eventually widens their horizon of knowledge and open doors for worldwide career opportunities.

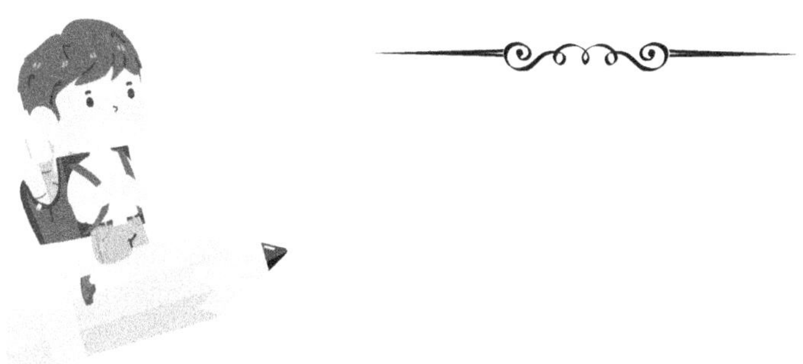

I'm Amritashaan. Language learning and teaching is my passion which keeps me occupied most of the time. As a person i'm modest and humble and firmly believe that life is a journey of souls; our body is a costume that it wears. Life is transient, Nothing is permanent. Let the soul enjoy its journey by doing some good deeds.

Amuse Consultants

easybreezyenglish4u@gmail.com

www.easybreezyenglish4u.com

About The Book

October 4, 2023
High Bands Practice

The book in your hand can give you a reason to cheer. Now writing a quality essay is no more a big deal. This book will guide you how to write a creative essay that should meet the standard set by the IELTS, PTE & TOEFL examination boards.

Moreover, all the essays in this book have been constructed personally by the author herself and they duly meet the requirements of the IELTS examination. The quality and the standard of the essays are up to the mark. They are written in such a manner that students can easily learn to improve their own essay writing skill. Some general tips for essay writing, impressive vocabulary and how to address different types of essays have spread on different pages which will make a reader breathe freshly in between. Once you master the art, you can excel in all essay writing exams.

HAPPY READING!

IELTS Writing - Assessment Criteria

Four Decisive Factors

- Task response
- Lexical resource
- Coherence and Cohesion
- Grammatical range and accuracy

Task Response is the first criteria of the four in the IELTS Writing Task 2 Band Descriptors and it is also one of the easiest criteria to score really well in. It means, **How well your answer answers the question.**

Lexical resource is all about how flexibly and fluently you can find the right words and phrases to convey precise meanings.

Cohesion refers to the connection of ideas from sentence to sentence. It deals with how your words and sentences link together. Broadly speaking, **coherence and cohesion** refer to the way a text is organized so that it can hold together.

This is a measurement of your ability to use **precise grammar** with a wide range of sentence structures without making grammatical errors.

SOME IMPORTANT THINGS TO KEEP IN MIND

- Essay writing is a formal writing.
- Do not use informal language. However, you are writing for an educated non-specialist audience. Therefore, your language does not need to be as formal as that of university essays.
- Do not use contractions like : don't, won't, he's, she's, can't, won't etc.
- Write do not, will not, he is, they have etc. instead.
- Learn the art of paraphrasing or use synonyms when possible. Never copy the question language while writing the introduction.
- Try to show range of sentences while writing. Complex, compound, passive, conditional type of sentences can take you an extra edge.
- Your language should make your point of view very clearly understood.
- The topics of the IELTS writing questions are supposed to be of general interest, and they claim that no specialist knowledge is required.
- Keep your essay well woven as your write up will also be examined in terms of coherence.
- Do not panic if you don't have ideas, even the best of language skills will not help you achieve your desired bands score.

IELTS Writing Test Tips

- Task 2 of the Academic Writing test is an essay.
- Read the question very carefully to understand what has been asked.
- Always take five minutes to first plan your answer before you start writing.
- When you write your answers, remember the examiners are grading you on your expression. There are no wrong or right answers.
- Examine the questions properly and see that you provide answer to all parts of the question.
- Remember to stick to the word limit. If you happen to write lesser than 250 in Task 2, you will lose marks.
- Always write the answers in your own language. If you use the words from the question exactly, you will not be given marks for the same.
- Arrange your basic ideas into different paragraphs. This shows the examiner how well you can organise your points.
- Always plan the structure of your essay beforehand.
- Make sure that you have relevant points to support the topic.
- Do not get deviated from the topic.
- Explain your ideas in different paragraphs and give a proper structured form to what you write.

IELTS Writing Test Tips

- Place a nice introduction, supporting ideas and real-life examples, followed by a conclusion.
- Do not puzzle yourself by writing long and complicated answers.
- Write well, coherent and organize your thoughts well.
- Make use of immaculate grammar. Grammar matters the most.
- Try to have five minutes in the end to review for any mistakes.
- keep the last paragraph for a valid conclusion of all the points you've made in the answer.
- Double check your answers for this common mistake.
- Remember, spellings are everything.
- Standard American, British and Australian spellings are all acceptable in IELTS.

IELTS – International English Language Testing System

LINKING WORDS FOR **IELTS** ESSAY WRITING

AMRITASHAAN

LINKING WORDS

Linking or transition words is a fantastic grammar and stylistic tool to make your writing more influential. They the words and phrases that connect your writing and help the reader form logical relationships between ideas. Remember that the linking words should come naturally as forcing a connector amid a sentence will result in an inexpert sentence composition.

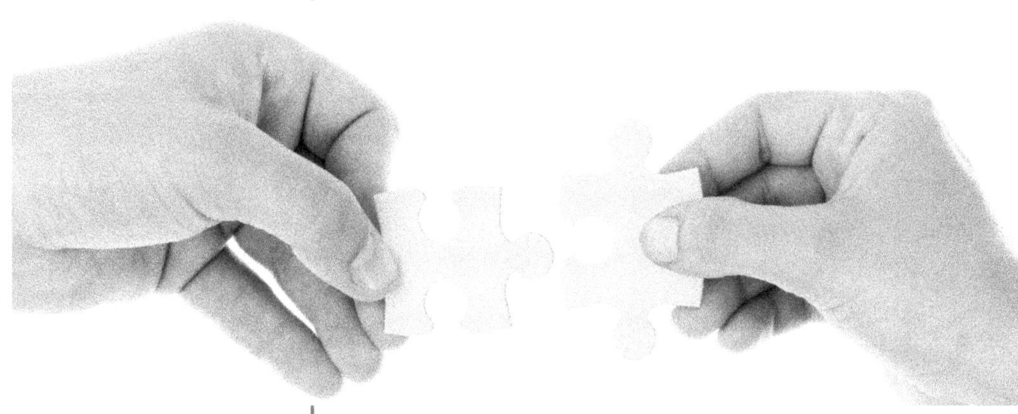

IMPORTANCE OF LINKING WORDS

IMPORTANCE
OF
TRANSITIONS

- Linking words make ideas more clear
- Show logical connection between sentences or paragraphs
- Help you write additional information to the main point
- Help you express consequences and results, causes and reasons, contrast and concessions etc.
- Make you write appropriate conclusion
- Make you achieve task requirement in terms of coherence and cohesion
- Make your essay internally well framed and rationally strong

Type of Essays

The IELTS Writing task 2 is considered as one of the most indulgent tasks across all other tasks by the IELTS aspirants. This task requires writing an essay encompassing various topics from all walks of life, right from social issues to workplace issues. These essays are of various types, including opinion essays, discussion essays, advantage-disadvantage essays, etc. The General and Academic Training Writing tests are usually graded to the same level. While IELTS Academic Writing test comprises topics suitable for undergraduate and postgraduate students, IELTS General Training module consists of excerpts on general topics from books, magazines, notices, company handbooks and guidelines that you are likely to face on a regular basis in an English speaking environment.

Academic & General Essay – Task : 2

Time Duration : 40 minutes
Word Limit : 250 minimum

STRUCTURE YOUR ESSAY

There are seven different types of essays that have been asked in the previous years of IELTS Exam. Though there are no hard and fast guidelines regarding the composition of IELTS Essay but organizing a structure helps in writing a methodological essay. An essay can be compiled in 4 paragraphs or more than 4 paragraphs. Each of the 7 type of questions requires a slightly different structure which you are going to get in different model answers.

An essay can be divided in different paragraphs starting with **Introduction** and ending with **Conclusion**. In between answering paragraphs can be according to the points you plan to explain.

Introduction

Paragraph – 1

Paragraph – 2

Paragraph – 3

Conclusion

Introduction

- Write a general statement on the question
- Reword / rephrase the question statement
- State what you are going to explain next

Paragraph – 1

- First idea to start with
- Your explanation to prove your point of view
- Some relevant example to support your answer

Paragraph – 2

- Second idea to start with
- Your explanation to prove your point of view
- Some relevant example to support your answer

Paragraph – 3

- Second idea to start with
- Your explanation to prove your point of view
- Some relevant example but mandatory

Conclusion

- Restate your answer, if required
- Summarize the main ideas

Planning is Important – IELTS Writing

The examiner needs to be able to understand what you are saying and see a clear progression of relevant ideas. Without a plan, this is difficult to achieve. Spending a few minutes planning your essay will give you an extra edge making your ideas more convincing and relevant.

High score in essay writing is easy if you plan your points/views before you start writing. Trying to write an IELTS essay without planning is just like going on a journey without a

map. You can have the most relevant ideas in the world but unless you can develop them into a well-structured essay, you may lose coherence and cohesion in your composition and it will affect your result. Make a brief plan and concentrate only on your planned ideas while writing.

○ _________
○ _________
○ _________
○ _________

How To Write an Introductory Paragraph

An introductory paragraph in very important for every essay you write. There is a very simple but effective technique to shape the opening paragraph. The skill can be achieved in three steps. You need to understand the meaning of Good Hook, Background Statement and Thesis Statement.

- Read the question very carefully
- Understand the main subject the question is on
- Think of some terse and telling sentence which is relevant to the question.
- Complete all important sentences for introduction carefully.
- Do not try to make your sentences very dense.
- Keep your language simple and clear but effective.
- Scan properly for any grammatical error.
- Write down in a beautiful handwriting.

Learn to write a good hook

You need to understand the question's key word and start your opening sentence with something clear, concise and catchy that makes examiner feel that you have given a right start.

Learn to write a Background Statement

The skill of paraphrasing will help you write your second sentence of opening paragraph. The information here should be broad but clearly focused and relevant to the question asked. The effective technique is to rewording is needed and you have to simply write the question sentence in your own words.

Learn to write a Thesis Statement

This is the third and the last sentence of opening paragraph. As there are different types of questions in IELTS Task 2, the thesis statement for every question changes according to the question asked.It is a statement in which you answer the question and make examiner know what you are going to write next. The sentence carries great importance in terms of TASK ACHIEVEMENT. The model answers to all more than 100 essays will make you understand the technique of writing Introductory Paragraph.

SOME GOOD WORDS

WRITE
DRAFT

ADVISE
COUNSEL

ADMIT
ACCEPT

ARGUE
QUIBBLE

COMMAND
AUTHORITY

BEHAVIOUR
DEMEANOR

START
OUTSET

LEGACY
HERITAGE

ACHIEVEMENT
ACQUISITION

DUTY
OBLIGATION

BURDEN
ONUS

PREVENT
AVERT

RESPECT
REVERE

MULTIPLY
MOUNT

DELIVER
TRANSPORT

Preface

A student is expected simply to state the advantages and disadvantages of some situation or trend being asked in the question.

Questions for IELTS advantages and disadvantages essays can be worded in some different ways.
Here is some typical wording that might be used :

- **What are the advantages and disadvantages of (some trend)?**
- **Do you think the advantages outweigh the disadvantages?**
- **Discuss the advantages and disadvantages and give your opinion.**

Though all the questions are basically same but learners are advised to write introduction and sum up as the question has been asked. Thus there remain slight differences when the answered is wrapped up.

1 **In some cultures, children are often told they can achieve anything if they try hard enough. What are the advantages and disadvantages of giving children this message?**

Within the realm of learning, childhood stands out as the paramount stage where various cultures instill in their young ones the notion that working hard can unlock endless possibilities. This thought process has both positive and negative effects on children, which I will discuss in the ensuing paragraphs.

First, based on the possible benefits, this teaching builds the self-confidence of the child from an early age and he understands the importance of diligence in life. Also, instead of being intimidated by a distant goal, children will get an optimistic mindset that improves their ability to achieve a goal. To illustrate, a newspaper survey showed that children who believed they could achieve a difficult goal were more successful than their peers.

In addition, the constructive spirit of the message makes them active and energetic where there is left no place for sluggishness and pessimism. They set their idols before them and put sincere endeavors towards their dreams. They push themselves up with a thought that those who try to climb the hill, they reach the summit.

Alternatively, the darker side of this thought process cannot be overlooked. First, in many situations, such teaching can create false expectations in children because they are not mature enough to understand the practical reality. Moreover, if children fail to achieve a goal after full commitment, they become prone to mental stress, which is not good for them.

All things considered, it is clear that this type of guidance undoubtedly makes children confident, active and intelligent from a young age and creates an optimistic approach, but one cannot ignore the danger of falling prey to false expectations, which eventually leads to depression and disillusionment in life.

- **Write introduction skillfully.**
- **Examine the question carefully and address every part of it.**
- **Do not copy the question language, use your own words exclusively.**
- **Organize your key points well and explain them suitably.**

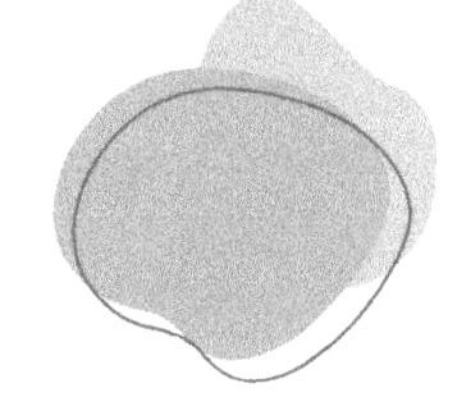

EASY TIPS
FOR
COMPLEX SENTENCES

Make use of 'because'

They are asked to play outdoor games **because** they have a very sedentary life.

Make use of 'since'

Scientists work in science **since** many things are yet to be explored.

Make use of 'after'

People buy products **after** they have read the reviews.

Make use of 'while"

Parents would work hard **while** their children continue their studies.

Make use of "until'

Practice more and more **until** you grow confident.

AMRITASHAAN

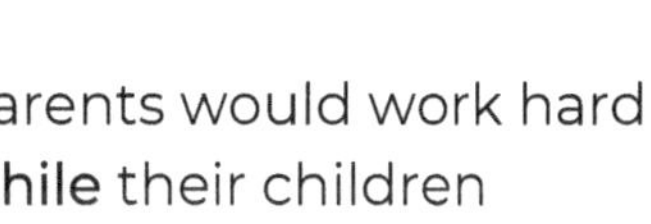

2 **People are encouraged to travel or work for one year after high school and before university studies. Write the advantages and disadvantages of this matter.**

Entering university has always been a long cherished dream of all school graduates. A contemporary smart practice which is in vogue these days is to motivate the students to travel or work for a period before their entry to universities. Both are the most imperative ways of accumulating the great practical lessons but its drawbacks are also worth considering.

To begin with the potential merits, travelling proves a boon for the students especially who are shy and introvert by nature as they grow confident in their behavior when they have to interact with new people during their travel, face new situations and exposure to the world outside their books takes them out of their shells.

In addition, a year travel broadens their horizon of knowledge in which they experience diverse cultures, lifestyles and develop a global mindset. Such exposure can lead to increase empathy and understanding of different perspectives, which in turn can make students more open and tolerant.

Then, working for a year too has its list of benefits which makes the students experience work market and they study what are the most demanding professional streams they should get trained in, in the university study. Additional income that students earn during the time alleviates the financial burden of their personal needs making them more prudent to understand the value of money.

On the flip side, some educators are dubious about the unperceived results of this practice. The small jobs they do hardly brings them any work experience and more seriously the high school graduates are too young to be exposed to the society as it is very hard for them to distinguish complex facts.

Furthermore, they are more likely to go astray due to many temptations all around and a long break of a year may off track them from their studies making them lose their interest in going back to their institutions.

In drawing things to a close, I believe that surely enormous are the benefits of inspiring students for travelling and work before their professional studies but it is important to keep in mind how it could be destructive too.

cherished dream, potential merits, diverse culture, global mindset, university study, additional income, financial burden, unperceived results etc.

Pick more Good Words for you

3 **Today more and more international sport events are organized in different countries. What are the advantages and disadvantages of hosting different international sporting events in a country?**

International sports events are measured as one of the most significant events worldwide. The trend of international tournaments has been in vivid rise in most of the countries round. In this essay, I am going to view both merits and demerits of international sport events on the host country.

Firstly, International sport events are an essential tool to elevate a country's image on a global platform as the events attract tourists from different parts of the world and host country gets an excellent opportunity to showcase its natural beauty, unique culture and infrastructure which makes it win the attention of the whole world. This could improve the country's international image and reputation.

Secondly, the influx of visitors brings with it an increase in tourism revenue which significantly benefits the host country's economy by generating great jobs opportunities and by improving the local trade. Tourists not only spend money on accommodation and meals but also on transportation, shopping, and entertainment. For example, three time more tourists to India were recorded during the last International Foot ball events in Mumbai.

Hosting a successful international event could create a sense of pride and patriotism among the citizens of the host country. There remains a vibe of jubilation among countrymen during such mega events which further serves as a platform for national unity making people feel proud of their country.

Focusing on the disadvantages, hosting these events can be incredibly expensive as infrastructures like sports arenas, accommodations, transportation and food facilities need to be built or upgraded to meet the standards of the event. If the cost of the event exceeds the budget, it may lead to economical imbalance. Seriously, since international sporting events tend to attract large crowds, which may cause traffic congestion and put a strain on public transport systems, can be very disturbing to the environment and local communities of a host country. The large influx of tourists can also put considerable pressure on the host country's natural resources and increase pollution levels.

In conclusion, international sports events have a significant impact on the host country as they serve as a catalyst for promoting country's profile, updating country's infrastructure and contribute to national pride and unity but its darker side requires contemplation too.

Use flawless grammar

EASY TIPS FOR COMPLEX SENTENCES

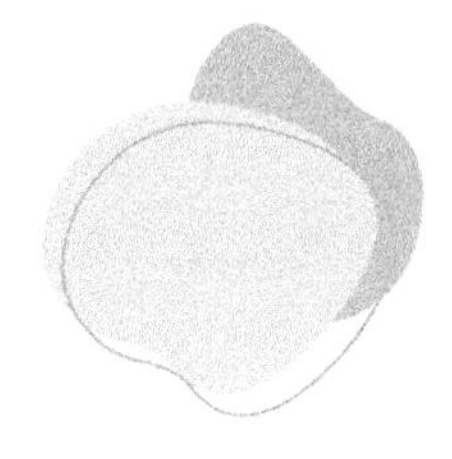

Make use of question words

Parents do everything **what** they find important for the healthy growth of thier kids..

Make comparison

The transportation facilities that we are getting today are **twice more** as better as people had a decade back.

Make Passive Sentences

Trees **are cut down** in the name of industrialization.

Give reasons

The people are running after more and more brands **due to the fact** that tagged products last long.

Show concession

Though there are many ways but punishment is the best alternative to ensure discipline on the roads.

AMRITASHAAN

4   **As air travel has become cheaper, more and more people are travelling abroad for their vacations instead of visiting places in their own country. Discuss the advantages and disadvantages of this?**

Air travel is one of the most desirable modes of travels not only for the people who are in good financial circumstances but also for those who belong to modest stratum of society. Since the air fares have plummeted, it is observed that travelling abroad during vacation for desirable destinations has gone more preferable than visiting native places. This has led to some great benefits but darker sides too need consideration.

The most potential merit is that cheap air travel has made it easier for middle class people to travel by air and connect with friends and family who live overseas. In the past, travelling to another country could be prohibitively expensive but now the facility is being availed even by a middle class.

In addition, it is also important to consider the economic benefits. Tourism is a major industry in many parts of the world and when more people are able to travel to different destinations; it can help support local economies. This can be especially important in developing countries, where tourism can be a major source of income for local people.

Finally, let us browse the possibilities with education and professional prospects. For example, Many employers today are looking for people who have international experience.

Whether it is studying abroad or networking with other professionals, travelling overseas can be a great way to improve career prospects and explore global market.

Looking at the other side of picture, cheap air travel is associated with crowding at airports, delayed flights, and long lines, all of which can be frustrating and stressful for travelers. Many times if travelers travel during peak season, they have to contend with overcrowded planes, limited air transport options etc.

Importantly, cheap air travel has led to an increase in tourism in many countries to an unmanageable level. While tourism can be a great source of revenue for these countries, it can also cause damage to the local environment and culture. The influx of tourists can lead to overcrowding, pollution, and strained resources.

Taking up as a whole, reasonable air fare has made travelling abroad possible for many. Whether it is for personal enrichment, economic development or career advancement, the benefits of travelling overseas are many and varied. Thanks to cheap air travel as more people than ever before are able to experience the joys of travel.

Comprehend Grammatical range and accuracy

5 **Introducing two or more foreign languages in the school curriculum has been in trend lately. Do you think the benefits of this trend outweigh its drawbacks?**

Language is a means of communication and so many languages are spoken around the globe by people of different nationalities. The practice of teaching foreign languages in school as a part of their syllabus is common. Introduction of a few oversea languages at academic level has both pros and cons which needs elaboration first.

Focusing on the potential merits, studying a foreign language is a fundamental element in building cultural proficiency. A language carries its culture, traditions, and values of the region where it belongs. Teaching foreign languages in schools exposes students to different cultures, customs, and beliefs. This exposure broadens the student's perspectives and encourages open-mindedness.

Counting next, mastering a foreign language can increase job opportunities. In the modern era of globalization, the world is moving towards a more interconnected and interdependent society where multinational companies are expanding their businesses worldwide and thus an understanding of foreign languages is becoming more critical. To exemplify, the trend of learning foreign language is in visible trend today among degree holders to find entry to international market.

Thus learning at school time is surely advantageous.

Evaluating the possible risks and drawbacks, it is feared that students may not have a natural aptitude for learning foreign languages or find learning it tedious. Learning a foreign language requires a lot of practice, memorization, and pronunciation. If the students are not motivated, it becomes challenging for them to master the language and thus teaching may not yield desired result.

Another noteworthy disadvantage of teaching foreign language at school is that teaching a foreign language tends to place a lot of emphasis on grammar rules and vocabulary memorization. It may result in limiting the study time of other essential subjects.

Time is a scarce resource in schools, and spending too much time teaching foreign languages can reduce the time available for other fundamental subjects. This can subsequently negatively affect students' overall educational outcomes.

In conclusion, teaching a foreign language at school presents both advantages and disadvantages. There is no denying the fact that its merits outshine the demerits as the practice broadens students' mindset for different languages and cultures around the world and importantly opens job opportunities for them in the international market.

6 **At the present time, the population of some countries includes a relatively large number of young adults, compared with the number of older people. Do the advantages of this situation outweigh the disadvantages? Give reasons for your answer and include any relevant examples from your own knowledge or experience.**

A country is comprised of the population of different age group people. Today it is documented that there are some countries around the globe which has significant number of young generation and in comparison the count of old populace is less. This situation surely carries both merits and demerits.

To unpack the advantages, a nation with considerable proportion of youth is believed to be a young nation where the people are active and energetic and full of passion to work. This young skilled workforce with their high spirits and enthusiastic efforts not only chase their dreams but their contribution makes their country progress leaps and bounds. For instance, it is a known fact that states with high proportion of young workforce show rapid development.

In addition, the young folk is equipped with latest knowledge and information and being progressive and innovative by nature, they have a say in the economical progress of a country. Besides being skilled labour, they add freshness in the society with their innovative ideas, they form the highest population of tax payee and thus builds economically strong society.

Every rose comes with a thorn. The greatest negative aspect is that the young population is a big liability on a nation where government has to be very vigilant to the susceptible needs of the youth. Like, unemployment can be a major issue. Generating job opportunities for millions of youth is not an overnight work.

Moreover the youth is immature, inexperienced want the best deal for everything like accessibility to the educational institutions, health care centers, public services etc. After that a little

discontent can make the frustrated youth revolt against government or jump in disconcerting anti-social activities leading to chaotic situations.

After considering pros and cons, I believe that advantages of having young population eclipses disadvantages as with young generation, a nation stays young, gets skilled workforce, innovative brains, a great energy where rapid progress makes a country economically well built.

7 **Consumer goods have become the most important part of people's lives. Do the advantages outweigh the disadvantages? Give reasons for your answer and include any relevant examples from your own knowledge or experience.**

Consumerism refers to the need of buying something that one already owns and undeniably such an urge is desperately felt by a present consumer. This concept of consumerism has both pros and cons which I would elaborate before reaching my answer.

On the positive side, consumerism plays a significant role in the economy of a country as people are made to spend willingly on different consumer goods which makes the money circulate and does not get stick in a few hands. In addition, there remains easy availability of everything like from kitchen spices to electrical vacuum cleaners etc. that is needed to make human life comfortable. Then after, it creates employment opportunities for the youth in market. Since demand of products rises extraordinarily with high consumption, companies hire more employees to meet the growing demand, leading to more jobs and income for individuals. Most importantly, consumerism eventually promotes competition among businesses and the sellers enhance their marketing efforts making people get best services.

However, the drawbacks are also worth considering.

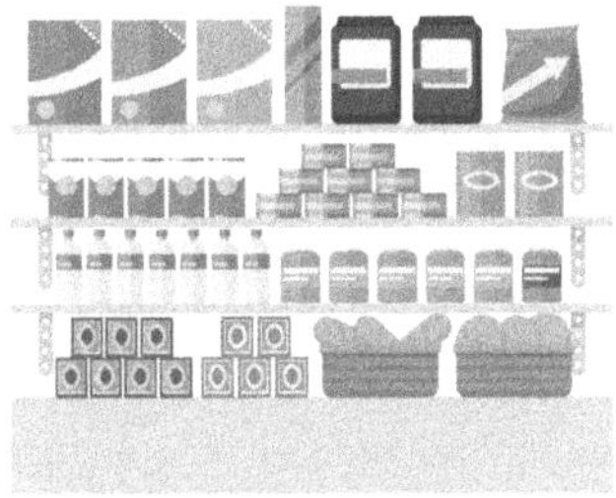

First, if there is excessive consumerism, people are more like to become sluggish or obese with their high dependence on the consumer goods. For example, who will walk to a little distant market when Uber taxi service is available.

Secondly, consumerism can be blamed for developing a materialistic culture and society that focuses on high quantity and costly goods rather than quality products. Status-conscious mindset often causes stress and anxiety. To make it more clear, like companies keep launching mobiles with new features at short intervals and a social status conscious person has to buy the new version though his old device still has no issue.

In conclusion, consumerism benefits and hurts societal ways of life. Love it or loathe it, we live in a world of consumerism which influences our lives in many way so it will not be wrong to say that its advantages outweigh the disadvantages.

Do not learn any essay. Plan your own ideas for every question to improve your writing skill.

8 **Today many people work in a group. Discuss the advantages and disadvantages of working in a group. Do you think advantages outweigh its disadvantages.**

A group means when a number of people are gathered, placed, or classed together for some purpose. Importance and need of group work has been recognized always and many works are accomplished by people in a group together. But certainly every aspect of life bears both positive and negative sides.

To begin with the advantages, people working together finish work more quickly and efficiently because not only work is divided amongst a number of people, instead of being handled by one person alone but also it allows more discussion and the opportunity to view issues from a variety of perspectives where all pros and cons are taken into consideration and the final outcome is always the best. Most importantly, if work is done in a group, it is more like to make all members share the duties equally. For example, a group is able to achieve something that each individual working alone might not be. There is a saying, " Many hands make work lighter."

Despite its benefits, group work can be one of the most stressful and emotionally exhausting part of one's life. A few disadvantages of group work are, there is the potential for personality clashes, which may hamper

Team work is the secret that makes common people achieve uncommon results

the ability to accomplish work in a timely and effective manner. Secondly, One person may take on more work than others. If someone does not do his fair share, the entire group has to bear the consequences. In the sports field, this may mean a defeat for the whole team. Thirdly, there is a well known saying, "Divided responsibility is no one's responsibility." So no one will do the job with good sincerity. Under such circumstances we can not expect satisfactory results.

To sum up, working in group is very common today. Though there are some demerits connected with it but I personally believe that advantages offset disadvantages as in a group, work can be finished fast, there remains high possibility of excellent results and work does not hang heavy on any one.

Think what makes you feel happy when you work in a group and what problems you face while working in a group. Your own ideas will enhance your writing ability.

SOME GOOD WORDS

ACCOUNTABLE RESPONSIBLE	**EMPHASIZE** TO PAY ATTENTION	**AMICABLE** FRIENDLY
PREJUDICE DISCRIMINATION	**DILIGENT** HARD WORK	**SHOWCASE** EXHIBIT
RUDIMENTARY PREPARATORY	**INEQUITABLE** UNFAIR	**INFEASIBLE** IMPRACTICABLE
INNATE INBORN	**DEPLETE** REDUCE	**IMPEDE** SLOW DOWN
SEDENTARY INACTIVE	**CIRCUMSPECT** CAREFUL	**AMELIORATE** MAKE BETTER

9   **Sending children to private schools than the government institutions is becoming more and more popular. What are the advantages and disadvantages of studying in private schools? Do you think that the advantages outweigh the disadvantages?**

Every parent desires to provide their children with the best of education but what makes them ambivalent is the choice of educational institutions. The most popular trend visible today is admissions in private schools instead of placing the wards in governmental run academic centers. The practice has both up and down sides which need detailed discussion before weighing high any option.

To initiate with, the greatest benefit of studying in private schools is that the students of private school reflect great confidence in communication with impeccable fluency in English language. The schools realizing the significance of global language, focus on making the learners understand it and conducive environment is created in the schools where all the students are advised to communicate in the language only. The students graduating from private school hardly face any language problem when they apply for jobs in multinational companies. To exemplify, studies reveal that English languages courses are generally joined by the students who come from government schools where their language of instructions was not English.

To add on, environment in which students are made to learn also matters the most. Gone are the day when children would learn in traditional classrooms of government aided schools where a teacher would read from books and write on black-boards. Modern highly educated parents find private schools the right places for their wards as smart classrooms with electronic boards, projectors, computers, e-study material, comfy sitting arrangement, a pleasant temperature, necessary lights, pure water, electricity, medical services, Internet services etc. facilitate a child with excellent learning experience.

Focusing on the dark side of private schools is the exorbitant fee structure which fleeces the parents of their hard earned money. Besides donations many funds are collected by the school managements in the name of developments and new infrastructure. In comparison, government schools fee pattern is so nominal that a labour man can also easily avail it for his child. For example, these eye-watering costs have trickled into the news headlines many times making it a matter of societal discussion.

In conclusion, there are both types of schools in society and they have their pros and cons but I tend to believe that acknowledging the need of good English level and importance of smart classes, the brighter side of private institution clearly dominates the negative aspect.

**Keep in mind
the word limit and must
meet it.**

10 **Traffic and accommodation problems are increasing and government should encourage businesses to move from cities to rural areas. Do the advantages outweigh the disadvantages?**

Heavy traffic on the roads and lack of residential places are the two different problems which are vividly on escalating scale mega cities. Expecting the impending danger, there comes a suggestion that the business organizations should be shifted to the rural areas away from the cities. The proposed trend wears pros and cons and they need to be elaborated before I reach my conclusion.

Focusing on the brighter side, firstly, it may relax the traffic problem as due to industrial activities hundred of vehicles keep running in the city streets. If the heavy loaded wagons instead of coming to cities, move on to the countryside, the city population is more likely to get relief from the daily hassles of traffic congestion. Instead of retarding the city traffic, these transportation vans will carry on their work on lonely lanes of remote areas.

Secondly, if the suggestion is implemented, it is also going to ease the problem of accommodation. Since, presently workers get workers' quarters near their industrial units which disconcertingly add to the problem high populations in mega cities. By transferring industrial unites away from cities will take the crowd of employees away to less populated areas.

For example, many temporary tent houses are setup by workers where they go for work and become the part of swelling population.

Turning the page, promoting industrialization in the countryside also carries some notable drawbacks. To begin with, presently the villages are heavenly places where people still breathe fresh air as nature has not been yet injured. By establishing factories in these areas, we are more likely to poison the air and pollute the water quality.

To add on, the countryside lane will die under the heavy burden of loaded dragons. Traffic jams will become the part of their life.

Last not least, deforestation will take place to provide shelters to the migrated labour.

In conclusion, moving business from cities to rural areas can be a brilliant decision in terms of finding solutions to the above said issues. However, there are disadvantages need to be measured meticulously against the advantages.

Practice formal language but avoid long convoluted responses.

EASY TIPS FOR COMPLEX SENTENCES

Make use of question words

The books **which** are composed by experienced writers are a great asset.

Make comparison

The **more** we work show concern, **the better** results we reach at.

Make Passive Sentences

More and more industries **are being set up** in the countryside today.

Give reasons

Because of heavy traffic, people get late to their place of work.

Show concession

Despite being an affluent nation, the grave health problems lie unattended.

AMRITASHAAN

Preface

The agree or disagree essay questions are the most commonly asked in the IELTS examination. They are also called as argumentative essays. In this type of essays, you are asked to give your opinion, whether you agree or disagree on the particular sentence that is given.

Here is some typical wording that might be used :

- **What do you think is right?**
- **What is your opinion about it?**
- **Do you agree or disagree with the statement?**

You are advised to either completely agree or completely disagree in this type of questions. In your introduction, you need to clearly state your position and then need to develop paragraphs elaborating your point of views.

11

As computers are being used more and more in education, there will be soon no role for teachers in the classroom. Do you agree or disagree with the statement?

A computer has brought a revolutionary transition in the field of education as nowadays, a comprehensively increasing number of students rely on computers for their studies. Undeniably, this changed scenario has brought a special concern regarding the possible decrease of importance of teachers in the classroom. I do not stand in accord with the expected fear.

To begin with, I opine, teachers who have been helping the students shape their future cannot be expected to lose their importance simply because of the introduction of computers in the schools. Their role in the class rooms is undeniably indispensible. As they know the learning capacities and the psychology of their pupils and thus guide and groom them accordingly by adopting different methods of teaching.

To add on, teachers develop emotional bond and take it as their moral responsibility to make their students practice repeatedly, correct their mistakes, make them know what is their strength and assist them in overcome their weakness. To make the point more clear, despite

"It's the teacher that makes the difference, not the classroom." –Michael Morpurgo

having all digital means, students still prefer being taught by the teachers.

Alternatively, a digital media no matter how effective it

may be, cannot be a replacement of a teacher in the class. Firstly, learning environment requires complete decorum but an electronic device can not ensure a sense of discipline, obedience, sincerity, regularity and spirit of learning.

Last not least, learners in the classes need complete curriculum to follow otherwise digital lessons may be confusing for them. A computing machine may occupy a little room in the class but class syllabus cannot work in the absence of a teacher.

To sum up, in the age of computers where technology is trying to dominate the field of education, I strongly reiterate that teachers' role can never fade away as teachers are the real guide, source of inspiration, course makers and their presence itself matters the most. Technology is only a helping device and certainly not an educator in itself.

Each body paragraph should present a reason for your view.

12

Modern medicine helps to live longer. Do you agree or disagree?

Modern medicine is a complex and multifaceted field that has revolutionized the way we approach healthcare. With advancements in medical technology, the quality of healthcare has improved significantly over the years, helping people to live longer, healthier lives. In this essay, I believe there is a great truth in the statement and my ideas will prove it.

Straight off the bat, I tend to believe that one of the most significant advancements in modern medicine has been in the field of immunizations. There was a time when toll of people would lose their lives in epidemics. Vaccines have been invented to eradicate many of the deadliest infectious diseases that once plagued humanity, including smallpox, polio, and measles. Thanks to vaccinations, we have been able to prevent countless illnesses and save millions of lives.

One another area where modern medicine has made great strides is in the diagnosis and treatment of diseases such as cancer. In recent years, we have seen a vast improvement in cancer survival rates, with more and more patients undergoing successful treatment and beating the disease. Medical professionals today diagnose the ailments and decide remedies and eventually bring the patient back to normal healthy life.

In addition, depression is believed to be one of the most deadliest of human mental disorders where suicidal tendency makes patients end their lives. Advances in neuroscience have led to a greater understanding of the brain and the intricacies of the mind, allowing the medicines to treat conditions such as stress, nervousness, depression and anxiety more effectively.

In conclusion, there is no denying the fact that modern medicine has had a profound impact on our lives, helping us to live longer, healthier, and more fulfilling lives than ever before. Whether through immunizations, cancer treatments, or geriatric care, medical professionals have helped to improve the quality of life for countless individuals.

Understand the use of Relative clause

One another area **where** modern medicine has made great strides is in the diagnosis and treatment of diseases such as cancer.

It is always good to make you point of view strong with some relevant example.

13   It is better for young to get advice from older people than young people. Do you agree or disagree?

Seeking guidance at an immature stage of life is quite common and the growing up people are advised to get directed in their life by the elderly folk and not from those who themselves are in the same phase of life. I personally support the intellectual assistance from older folk.

To begin with, we should listen to our elders not because they are always right but because they have more experience in being wrong and thus they are in better situation to offer us priceless wisdom.

In addition, patience, steadfastness, emotional firmness etc. are some important attributes of the old age which further assures the best counseling. Every issue is prudently analyzed by them and our steps are put on in the right directions.

For example, if one is seeking help regarding the down phase of life, he would not only get how to deal with the situation but an elderly fellow will also morally guide him about the ups and downs of life which are an integral part of life.

Alternatively, the advice from youngsters is not recommended assuredly as they themselves are inexperienced and unproven. How can a young man guide his friend about his future as he himself has not gone through the age.

Moreover, intolerance, impatience, egoism, arrogance are the traits which keep him excited and for lack of far off vision, they cannot be the perfect guide. A young friend may advise his friend to fight and take revenge in some situation, whereas a senior will always ask to believe in forgiveness and get off the high horse and learn to be kind and humble.

To sum up, this is quite acceptable that the people with best advice are usually the ones who have been through the most and undoubtedly our elders like parents, teachers, grandparents etc are one of those. Their guidance will be valuable as they are mature and seen the world where as the young folk may lack that far-off insight.

- Elderly folk has experience of being wrong
- They analyze everything wisely.
- Young friends are unproven
- They lack far off vision.

GOOD WORDS

Intellectual, attribute, steadfastness, inexperienced etc. Pick good words from every essay and add to your vocabulary.

14 It is good for school and university students to take part in part-time jobs. Do you agree or disagree?

Education time is quite crucial stage in students' life where they are expected to devote their all time to studies only. But now as followed in many countries, the new concept is to encourage children for part time jobs. My perception makes me believe that there can be many good aspects if this practice is promoted.

I attempt to explicate that taking part-time jobs benefits young people enormously as it helps students put theories, they have learnt into practice and gain precious working experience. In today's job market, employers not solely focus on the academic skills, but also put more attentions on experience. They prefer the students who can practically perform the tasks.

Likewise, being in a work place, a learner finds himself in a world that is totally different than his bookish web. Here he comes to know what is communication, self-management, interpersonal skills and team spirit, which are treated as crucial practical skills in employment. Noteworthy point is, books only fills mind with knowledge but how to use that knowledge comes with job experiences only.

To add on, being a student usually means little or no money, but when one is working part time, he no longer has to worry about being able to afford the basic essentials or relying on parents funding to get by. One can start affording little luxuries like going out with friends and treating himself to something nice and seriously one can even use his little pay for his mobile recharge or tuition fee.

Continuing with more pros, early employment is a boon for those students who are shy and introverted by nature.

A part-time job helps them to come out of their shell and aids in growing their confidence when they are forced to communicate with different personalities and improve their communication skills and make them peep into the professional world, their final destination.

To sum up, keeping in view all the wonderful outcomes, it becomes easy to conclude that students' involvement in part-time jobs is a welcoming

idea as it cultivates sound interpersonal skills and puts students on the top in the job market among the crowd of applicants.

- **Write your essay in a formal manner**
- **Organize your essay in different paragraphs**
- **Make use of words you are familiar with**
- **Do not repeat words and ideas**
- **Do not force memorized vocabulary in your essay**
- **Use neutral tone of writing**

It is necessary for parents to attend a parenting training course to bring their children up. Do you agree or disagree?

Parents are believed to have the responsibility to bring up their children in the best possible way and it is considered to be quite obligatory for parents to get the training to be the best parents. I am of the opinion that effective parenting can surely be the key to raise a child in the best manner.

First of all, if we talk about a new born baby, since he is entirely at the mercy of his parents, it is highly essential to help a child develop healthy and such training courses make the parents know how to handle this soft, tender bundle of life for his daily routine, about a child's daily diet plan and importantly, about all the vaccination, drops and doses programs, where a child is protected against the diseases like polio, measles, influenza, hepatitis etc. Besides this, parents are educated how their child can go cripple for whole life if the doses are not injected in time. Most of the medical surveys reveal that generally the polio child suffers are from the stratum of the society where parents were not educated or ignorant about the immunization schedule of the child.

My second thought says, a parent may be academically highly qualified but he hardly knows how to deal with a child during various problems associated with the kid. Like a toddler's thumb sucking, hitting, fighting with the siblings, not getting chores done, behaviour problems, discipline problems, temper tantrums etc make parents nag and they yell at little ones. It is natural to feel annoyed at a child's disruptive behavior but parenting lessons are more like to guide them how to react, how to face that particular situation which may also help child get positive lesson.

In conclusion, I firmly recommend parenting training courses as 'What you sow so shall you reap' a common saying remind us the same fact. A trained parent will surely give healthy life to his child with good knowledge regarding a child's early care and issues related with growing up tenure.

Shyness
Impulsivity
Inability to pay attention
Lack of time management skills
Mood swings
Destroying own things
Bullying others
Arguing with others
Blaming others for their own faults
Constantly talking
Reluctant to participate in activities

16 **It is not necessary to travel to other places to learn about other cultures of other people. We can learn just as much from books, films, and the internet. Do you agree or disagree?**

A man always wears an insatiable desire to explore the world to quench his thirst of learning more and more about different cultures, customs and traditions of the people living in different parts of the earth. Though in the present time of technology this search has gone very feasibly easy with the use of different modes available like online surfing, brochures, magazines but I personally stand in the favour or visiting places in hunt of knowledge.

To begin with, there is a famous saying that the world is like a book, those who do not travel, read only one page of it. One of the benefits of travel is the opportunity to have new experiences and witness different cultures. One gets a chance to interact with the people and who knows when and where one gets an inspirational tint to bring an exceptional transformation in life.

Importantly, numerous are the living styles around the ball, Sightseeing and experiencing the local cultural can expose us to local art, music, cuisine, architecture etc. and the list goes on. Many travelogues reveal that many travelers use the occasion to actively learn new skills by joining their classes and become the part of their traditional activities. Thus all these benefits can be reaped only

by joining their classes and become the part of their traditional activities. Thus all these benefits can be reaped only by those who wander around the world.

On the flip side, if I talk about cultural information by reading books, browsing websites etc. it would only be a grapevine report, a hearsay.

Undoubtedly, it will also add to our knowledge and keep us informed about great things but the weather of that particular place a traveler may enjoy, the music a tourist may listen and get fascinated, the food a visitor may relish and feel ecstatic and other holistic experiences of life etc. are not rewards a reader can reap. Last not least, knowing about different conventions, prevailing trends, traditions through others' perception

may give blurred and incomplete picture of some incredible life.

To conclude, earning cultural knowledge may be possible by other ways but I personally do not agree that travelling is not required for the same purpose. The real life experience in many things, familiarity with the people, their traditions, chances of getting motivation and first hand view of the world are some reasons which compel me to disagree with the given statement.

SOME GOOD WORDS

PERPETRATE
COMMIT

DELIBERATELY
PURPOSELY

MONOTONOUS
DULL

PRECARIOUS
DANGEROUS

RENOWNED
FAMOUS

PROCURE
ACQUIRE

INDISPENSABLE
VITAL

FEEBLE
WEAK

GLIMPSE
LOOK

CONCEPT
IDEA

SNAPPY
RAPID

COMMENCE
INITIATE

SERENE
PEACEFUL

OBESITY
OVERWEIGHT

UNPRECEDENTED
UNPARALLELED

17 **Nowadays it is common for people to get married and have children in their thirties rather than when they are younger. Do you agree or disagree that this trend will benefit society?**

Matrimony is considered the most significant event in one's life. Gone are the days when people would jump into the relation quite early in their life but in the present time, it is mostly children reach their thirties when they start their family life. I personally find the trend quite favorable for the society.

To begin with, a society prospers and progresses provided that the people live in harmony and happily they take care of their family units. Late marriages ensure maturity which is highly needed requisite for stable relations. By the time they realize that this relation can be reared great respect, love and understanding. Having

being reached an adult age, the couple is more like to share their responsibilities in good accord and enjoy the bliss of relation.

In addition, by the time they get financially settled in their life by entering professional arenas. Monetary security is one another factor for successful and contented married life with no cases of separations or daily disputes because of poor living standard. Even the statistical reports reveal that number of divorces is drastically higher among early marriages which affect the healthy fiber of the society.

Focusing on the other fact which states that couples

have their children in thirties, can also be listed as good for society as this is the stage, they do not take their new born as a burden on them.

Admittedly, the quality of parenting a child receives, plays a major role in his comprehensive development. Giving birth to a child is not the issue but how his physical, mental, emotional and academic needs are regulated, matters the most. Only mentally, emotionally and financially well settled parents can handle the affairs reasonably way.

To sum up, I firmly find the statement acceptable and complimentary for the society. The trend of getting married late and thus having babies in thirties will have good impact on society as the

mature couples will have long lasting relations, the divorce cases will turn down and importantly the couples will be able to give society fit and fine members.

Make use
of
Subordinating conjunctions
-
although, provided that,
rather than,
in order to

18 **Some people say that all popular TV entertainment programs should aim to educate viewers about important social issues. Do you agree or disagree with this statement?**

Since television is one of the most influential mediums to reach the masses, it is suggested that social issues should be brought to light by this entertaining industry through their daily soaps. I personally believe that such noble suggestions can certainly help in eradicating social issues persisting in the society.

To begin with, discussion and debates on social issues at various platforms are extremely important. There are so many issues like poverty, discrimination, immigration, domestic violence, unemployment, women safety, sanitation facilities etc. which some may be facing and many may not be even aware of. If television programs focus on them, the unseen face of the society will be unveiled and the viewers will think critically about the concerning issues.

In addition, it is an accepted fact that millions of people believe and follow what they see in variety of programs daily. They feel themselves connected with the characters portrayed on the screen. The character who may be a simple man struggling to achieve his aim or a participant of some entertaining reality show exhibiting his talent, can become a source of motivation for millions of viewers. For example, a television serial 'Flight' educated thousands of girls to educate themselves to become financially independent.

Furthermore, since this is a media that already has big audience so the platform if used well can do wonders. Bringing change in mindset of people is not easy but positive messages can be easily spread across the country through recreational dramas.

To end up, television can play a crucial role in making people aware of social concerns, if the programs are picturized in the way that makes the viewers aware of serious matters, enlightened audience will grow sensitive to find some solution and the great objective of television programs will be achieved.

Understand the use of Relative Clause

The character who may be a simple man struggling to achieve his aim or a participant of some entertaining reality show exhibiting his talent, can become a source of motivation.

19 **Some people think it is ok for adults to play computer games. Do you agree or disagree? Why? Include specific details to support your answer.**

Video games have often suffered from an unfair perception that they are solely the domain of young children, teenagers, and young adults. However a section of people opine that it is acceptable if elderly folk pick up a controller and engage in gaming. I too find the idea to be good enough for adults, as they can help adults in many ways.

The first and foremost idea that I can put forward is, virtual games can be a great way for adults to get away from their distress after a long working day. Instead of idling away time on a lazy afternoon, if they engage themselves in some key board game, they will not only enjoy the fun but will get a new vibe of freshness and happiness in their monotonous life.

Another benefit of gaming for adults is the potential to strengthen relationships with their children or younger relatives. By understanding the games and the culture surrounding them, it can help facilitate conversations and build a bond between generations. For example studies reveal that parents who are acquainted with the video games keep better check on their children and also allow them time for the same.

Continuing with positive aspects, the life of adults sometimes go quite isolated as they hardly get time for socializing but computer games make them win new friends. Many games are designed with multi-players, allowing adults to not only play with family members or friends, but also meet new people from around the world with shared interests.

Last not least, engagement of adults in computer games is fine it can be a form of learning technology. Since life has gone totally technical today with the advent of various devices for daily use, adults sometime feel themselves outdated for new technology. Use of joy sticks, remote controls, key boards etc. help them learn all new features and thus there is nothing wrong if our parents or grandparents enjoy these games.

In conclusion, despite the belief that computer games are just for young people, they can provide a wide range of benefits for individuals of all ages. The people who are adults should feel free to engage in gaming as a way to unwind their stress, strengthen relation with young generation, meet new people and importantly a way to learn how to use new technology.

20

Museums and art galleries will not be needed because people can see historical objects and works of art by using a computer. Do you agree or disagree with this opinion?

Technological innovations with which it has gone possible for a man to have a tour of any place, he wants, has made one assume that institutions like museums and art galleries are not necessary places as having panorama or knowledge about them is accessible through virtual tours online. While there is no denying the likelihood of virtual cultural access but I vehemently negate the idea that these establishments will not be in need in coming time.

To begin with, I believe, it is important to understand the significance of physical structure of museum and art galleries which serve great purpose.

Like, a trip to a museum is a unique experience that one cannot visualize until the place is visited by one. Museums are typically packed with rich history, unique artifacts, and thought-provoking exhibitions which make the visitor peep into the real facts of life that they knew from books. First hand view of ancient old objects like attires, swords and spears etc. of emperors provides such an unusual experience that one feels the presence of history or get to know about the evolution of society. The whole environment provides exciting and thrilling experience which no virtual tour can replace.

Moving ahead, inspite of many online applications, a visit to these structures is an education in itself as they are the store house of important educational resources. By visiting these institutions, we can have the glimpse of unprecedented past and can learn about history, culture in an interactive and engaging way. An extensive collection of artworks, such as paintings, sculptures, photographs and installations that showcase different styles, themes, and techniques widen the horizon of knowledge.

The ambience, aroma of the place, personal touch, emotional impact and cultural contexts that a visit to these institutions provide are unmatched with virtual tours.

To sum up, visiting a museum virtually may sound like a great idea for many reasons but I firmly hold an opinion the significance of these institutions will always be felt. The experience and knowledge one can have by going to the places is unparalleled as technology cannot create the real scenario.

**Practice variety
of
question types
&
Get Feedback**

Preface

It is really common to see 'To what extent...' essay questions in an exam. They come up time and time again with across a range of different subjects.

Well, this type of question allows the student to show a variety of skills. The students are at their liberty whether to totally agree or stand just contrary to the given statement.

Most importantly students can also display independent judgment by analyzing the importance of different pieces of information.

EASY TIPS
FOR
COMPLEX SENTENCES

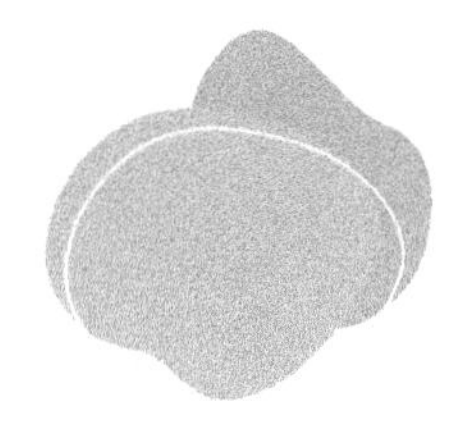

Make conditional sentences

If rules are made strict, the situation will improve.

Make Use of Time Linkers

While buying things online, people ignorantly save their PIN numbers and face issues later.

Make Passive Sentences

Fast food **should be avoided** by people to enjoy a healthy life style.

Use the 'ing' form to start sentences

Guiding youth may seem difficult but fact is that they are still innocent and depend on their elders for important decisions.

Make Contrast

Old education system is producing excellent brains. New system **however** is still the need.

AMRITASHAAN

21

Media and newspaper show vulgar crimes on news, which cause fear and provoke culprits. Some people think that crime news on TV should not be telecast. To what extent do you agree or disagree?

We are quite often faced with the appalling stories of crimes that take place in one part of country or other and these stories often dominate the news. Intellectuals of society are not in the favour of telecasting or publishing of such news for it could trigger the feelings of anxiety or could lead to further hike of violent behavior. I find the fear to be quite genuine but personally believe in the coverage of such news.

The thinkers of society opine that horrifying news can be incredibly disturbing and traumatizing for viewers, especially those who may have experienced similar situations. We often hear stories of people being attacked or raped in seemingly safe places such as parks, or even at home. This makes people feel scared that these thing could happen any time anywhere.

To make it more clearly, in metro cities parents do not allow their daughters to be outdoors till late in the evening for the fear of some mishaps.

In addition, the news can also provoke the culprits to commit more misdeeds as the evil doers become emboldened that they can continue to commit similar crimes without getting caught. Many times the news stories work as a coaching sessions for potential criminals and their evil plans are designed in the same way.

At the same time, I think, different news media are responsible for ensuring that citizens are informed about what is happening in the vicinity around. Reporting on vulgar crimes can help to raise awareness about safety issues making people more vigilant.

Last not least, it may also work as a warning for the culprits that their evil plans will not be allowed to work and severe punishments will await for them otherwise.

To encapsulate, undoubtedly, though the horrifying news can be disturbing but reporting on them serves greater purpose as it enlightens the public, goes like a warning to the offenders and thus keep people vigilant about their safety.

Try Making More Sentences
of
Subordinating Conjunctions

Although crime news create a feeling of terror among the viewers, the telecast is imperative as general awareness makes people aware of evil happenings in the vicinity.

22

Doing an enjoyable activity with a child can develop better skills and more creativity than reading. To what extent do you agree? Use reasons and specific examples to explain your answer.

Parents always strive to incorporate creative spirit into their children's lives but remain dubious which is more important fun activity or habit of reading. It is observed that introduction of enjoyable activity into the lives of children is more agreeable to foster creativity and skills than asking them to read. I personally believe that pleasing activities unquestionably are essential for kids but significance of reading can also not be overlooked.

To begin with, it is generally seen, fun activities provide a favorable environment where a child improves their different skills. Like, as he gets into an environment where there is no restriction and where a child is like a free bird. He does whatever he wants to do and becomes more communicable and learn to express himself. The studies reveal that with involvement in fun activities, even an introvert child comes out of his shell of shyness.

To add on, running and chasing games help them improve their overall mental health, promoting healthy habits such as self-discipline, a good attitude and healthy relationships with others. Most importantly, now he is enlightened with the importance of people around him and he not only enjoys the company of his near dear ones, understands the sweetness of relations but also learns to be social in his life.

One another fact is that if such a relaxed atmosphere is created where their brains work freely, the kids are more likely to explore many possibilities and look at the world with their own eyes. The freedom to explore allows children to experiment and they come up with new solutions to their problems. To exemplify, Simple tasks like playing with clay or building a sand castle can help children develop critical thinking skills.

Alternatively, I personally believe, reading too has its un-disputable role in children's life. Reading is a great source of entertainment and learning by which a child's imagination is fueled. With each new story, characters, and scenarios a child is exposed to the world. As children read, they start creating their own imaginative world and thus go creative in their life.

To put everything in a nutshell, a child's comprehensive development depends on many factors in which enjoyable activities and reading collectively play a vital role and develop many above mentioned skills among children and also make them creative.

**Learn more phrases
for
Lexical Structure**

**imagination is fueled.
imagination is blazed.
imagination is ignited.**

23

International sporting events promote peace between countries. To what extent do you agree or disagree?

International sporting events have long been praised for promoting peace, tolerance and understanding between nations. Though there are great chances of cooling down the relations of countries at international level but an environment of uneasiness it creates can also not be overlooked.

To begin with, it is assumed that international sporting events are an excellent platform for promoting peace and establishing stronger relations between nations. When people from different countries come together to compete, they share a sense of excitement, they create a bond based of mutual respect and understanding, better get to know that people across boundaries almost have same fair share of joys and sorrows, same struggle to survive, same hope and aspirations which breaks down barriers between nations and build bridges of communication and collaboration.

Furthermore, they provide an opportunity to showcase the positive values of sportsmanship, teamwork, and fair play which have the potential to promote peace. One significant example of the power of sporting events to promote peace is the Olympic Games. They provide a model how nations can work together to build a peaceful global community.

Alternatively, I fear that these events may create an atmosphere of tension as one of the most troubling aspects of events is the way in which the athletes and fans exhibit their emotions and a sense of pride for their country which many times escalate into animosity and aggression towards other nations. Every country and each player participates with the intention to win as their nation's reputation remains at stake. Their principles of sportsmanship take wings no sooner did they lose the match. Their blatant show of outrage, absurd language and open challenges to the judges' decisions not only spoil the charm of the event but sows the seed of poison between the two nations

To wind up, International sporting events have been heralded as a means to promote global peace. However, upon closer examination, it becomes clear that these events though create an environment of mutual understanding but do not always succeed in their intended purpose.

SOME GOOD WORDS

AFFLUENT WEALTHY	VERITABLE UNQUESTIONABLE	**ELITE EDUCATED**
LUCRATIVE BENEFICIAL	INSURMOUNTABLE IMPOSSIBLE	**DENOUNCE CONDEMN**
SKEPTICAL DOUBTFUL	**VICISSITUDES ALTERATIONS**	**BACKLASH REACTION**
VEHEMENTLY STRONGLY	**GLEAN GATHER**	**REPERCUSSION CONSEQUENCE**
ONUS BURDEN	**APPARENTLY EVIDENTLY**	**SOPORIFIC DULL**

Recent figures show an increase in violent crime among youngsters under the age of 18. Some psychologists claim that the basic reason for this is that children these days are not getting the social and emotional learning they need from parents and teachers. To what extent do you agree or disagree with this opinion?

It appears that the youth crime rate in the modern world is increasing at an alarming rate. Although there may be many factors causing this issue, it is perceivable that the absence of suitable education provided by parents and teachers are the major problems behind sorry affair. This position will thus be analyzed in the following paragraphs, supported by relevant examples.

Firstly, parents' increasing occupational commitments have limited their opportunities to educate children on moral qualities. The current economic condition of the contemporary society requires parents to spend more time at work.

This has consequently created fewer interactions between children and parents, precluding youngsters from learning basic emotional aspects such as love and affection from adults.

An exemplary case can be seen from an unruly brat, who barely gets a chance to learn about a specific manner to talk to strangers or elderly people. Hence, it seems that such reality has disabled him to possess an ethical mindset, which might case behavioral problems outside home.

Secondly, the modern education system enforces students to work for exceptional achievements, rather than ethical perspectives. instead of instilling the feelings of co-existence and co-operation, the students are made to compete and out do others and such an environment generates animosity among them.
It is personally felt that such an inappropriate teaching has left many students to focus on achieving material accomplishments devoid of any gentle concern for their fellow mates in the society.

In conclusion, the two aforementioned ideas clearly encapsulate how the lack of solid and ethical supervisions by adults leaves children to develop problematic thoughts and behaviour.

Practice a variety of Sentences

Parents **rather than** providing time to their wards are more engaged in their professional pursuits. Children get to know about family relations and culture **provided that** parents spare ample time for them.

25

Today, the high sales of popular consumer goods reflect the power of advertising and not the real needs of the society in which they are sold. To what extent do you agree or disagree that advertisements make us buy more ?

Advertising is a modern phenomenon for commercial success which is used to attract the attention of prospective customers to a business or its products or services. Some market analysts insist modern commercials are actively interfering with buyer's desires, developing artificial needs and this becomes quite evident because of the escalating sale of the consumer goods. I cannot give my consent to the statement as I have some reasons to prove my point of view.

To begin with, consumers do not always succumb to the temptation of advertisements. Advertisements only provide consumers with information about the goods. In fact, modern buyer is wise enough to consider several factors, for instance, price, their necessity and the quality of the product before they make any purchase. The consumer's buying decisions largely depend on his choice and financial condition. For example, an affluent buyer is not going to order a bathing soap because its hype has advertised that the soap fairs the skin.

There is another strong reason to prove it, the sale of products which are popular in the market is completely attributed to the demand of it. This is because necessity is superior to any other features. For example, an emergency drug is not purchased by a customer on the basis of any advertisement. Similarly, we can see the sale of petroleum products such as gasoline, which are neither influenced by adverts nor by any price hike. People buy them because they need them.

To sum up the foregoing, I feel it hard to blame the commercials for luring the customers unnecessary as the modern buyer intelligently consider the price, his need and most importantly his finances, before putting anything in his cart.

Understand the Structure

of

the sentences

The sale of products which are popular in the market is completely attributed to the demand of it

26

Some people say now there is less communication between family members than in the past. To what extent do you agree or disagree?

A family is believed to have woven in a fine fiber if there are regular interactions between the members of a family. With so much vivid socio-technical transitions in the society, it is opined by some folks that communication among parents and siblings relatively has gone down. The things were different in the recent past. I feel it difficult to agree with the statement and I have reasons for the same.

To raise my first reason, I would say that today people are reaping the benefits of technology. Undeniably, people have got highly occupied in their personal and professional pursuits, having no time to sit and chat with their relatives, but modern technological tools have made it possible not only the family units but the friends and folks to have good interaction with all they need.

There would be no exaggeration in saying that presently not only the family but we have extended families and friends and applications like Facebook, Whatsapp, Google meet, Instagram etc. keep us in touch with all those who are in our list.

Quite interestingly, a son in hurry may forget to inquire about his parents well being in person before leaving for his workplace in the morning but in his family social media group he will surely be in touch with them the whole day.

Audio – video features with no calling cost has made people interact more.

Additionally, Out of sight, out of mind, proverb hardly wears significance today. A family member today may be at Mars or seven seas away, internet technology, telephones etc. keep everyone connected. Gone are the days when while flying abroad children would hug their parents in emotions not knowing when they would get a chance to see them again. Today minute to minute updates are being shared and there is no feeling that anyone is away.

Closing the article, I would say there is nothing to think passive, family members even today are indulging in good communication and surely getting and giving time to one another. The only difference is that the mode of communication has changed.

Do not make use of the words, you do not know the meaning of. The examiner is not expecting English scholar's level language proficiency from you !

27

Soon people who cannot work with computers will be disadvantaged. To what extent do you agree or disagree with idea?

Information technology has brought sweeping changes in people's life and excessive use of computers in different fields creates a belief that non-computer users will experience a huge drawback sooner or later. The fear may wear some truth but I personally believe that non computer savvy will still survive in the society.

Talking about the apprehension, almost every job requires the proper use of these machines. For instance, many job postings indicate computer proficiency as one of the mandatory requirements. It is, therefore, evident that people who lack such skills are deprived of vast job opportunities. If we talk about the contemporary education system which solely depends on technology and any individual with no knowledge of computer will not be hired as a teacher as he will not be able to create virtual lessons.

Moreover, the world is gradually moving towards digitalization in all sectors. It may be keeping office records, making study lessons, issuing identity documents, charting designs of building or scanning inner parts of human body etc. every field requires the device with its application. A clerk, a teacher, a doctor, an engineer or even a shop keeper trading good need to know how to use this technology. As a result, it is acknowledged that one who is not techno-savvy, will sit idle.

However, I believe that some individuals may not have the capability to work with computers, this does not mean that these people are incapable of securing employment.

Though, older individuals may not be well acquainted with digital working, their years of work experience could be an asset. There are many jobs which require creativity, communication skills, ethical knowledge, counseling skills, technical skills that do not involve computers or any device. Personal competence and skills in different fields will help many earn their bread and butter respectfully.

In conclusion, undeniably most service providers may have embraced technology to enhance efficiency and timeliness in service delivery but still many who are not technology literate will find their way to work for sure but trying to get familiar with computers can be recommended.

Use suitable phrases for important words
Like : Disadvantaged
Go out of job
Sit idle
will have no fish to fry
will lose their usefulness
will be of no worth

 Smoking not only harms the smoker but also those who are nearby. Therefore, smoking should be banned in public places. To what extent do you agree or disagree? Give reasons for your answer and include any relevant examples from your own knowledge and experience.

Smoking is a widespread and dangerous habit that affects millions of people worldwide. Despite the fact that smoking is not only injurious to the smoker but also to others who are nearby, many people still continue to smoke publicly. Therefore, I firmly opine that banning smoking in public areas is a crucial step towards ensuring the protection of the general public.

One of the main reasons why smoking should be banned in public areas is the ill effect it has on people's health. People who do not smoke but they become passive smokers and are exposed to the same harm as those who smoke directly. This exposure can cause respiratory problems, such as asthma and bronchitis.

For example, according to the research of American Cancer Society, a pregnant mother may face the problem of miscarriage or pre-mature labour if her husband is in the habit of smoking.

Another reason why smoking should be prohibited in public areas is the negative impact it has on the environment, air goes smoky and people complain of suffocation. If cigarette butts make up a significant part of litter on streets, sidewalks, and parks, they are more likely to reach water sources with its toxic components causing harm to wildlife and ecosystem.

Last not least, exposure to cigarette smoke in public places can perpetuate negative behavior among young generation leading them to addition. Children who witness adults smoking in public may perceive this behavior as socially acceptable, leading them to experiment with smoking themselves at a young age.
For instance, innocent children many time pick up thrown away butt of cigarette and imitate the smokers.

To recapitulate, since smoking is injurious to the health may be of smoker or non-smoking people around. It will be an appreciable step if it is strictly not permitted in public area as the non smokers will not be affected, environment will remain undamaged and most importantly little children will not get exposed to such undesirable habits.

You can have your perception for any question and can write accordingly. Importantly point is to make your ideas relevant and convincing.

Although there is a lot of translation software available, learning a language still could be advantageous. To what extent do you agree or disagree? Give reasons for your answer and include any relevant examples from your own knowledge and experiences.

Communication with the people of different languages is not a big task today as many translating applications make it possible. Though the translating tools may be helpful but still learning a language is believed to be more conducive. I find the statement agreeable and I have reasons to prove my perception.

I believe, despite the availability of translating machines like Google translator or Talk talk etc. learning foreign languages is still required as it would serve great purpose. Communication with people in their language not only removes the language barrier but makes a person more acceptable in the society. The language proves favorable in terms of understanding the rituals, culture and tradition of that particular place.

Adding to it, knowledge of language opens many opportunities for people as they can be hired by multinational companies provided that the applicants must be a polyglots.

Focusing on other reason, language learning is highly recommended to the learners going to foreign countries for their higher studies as if they do not know the language, they are not expected to achieve their aims.

The most significant example is that English, French, Dutch etc. languages courses are completed by students before they fly for international colleges and universities.

Now it is also necessary to understand why inspite of having wonderful translating software available, one cannot rely on the device exclusively.

First, every language has its own idiomatic expressions, regional variations, linguistic quirks which a machine can never understand. Like words can be translated but not the whole speech with exact meaning and tone a speaker wants to convey.

Translating software remains imperfect in terms of translating accurately in the target language. Most importantly, a machine fails to express the emotions like whether the things have been said in anger, love or in a lighter vein.

Last not least, even if all drawbacks are ignored, would it be possible to open translating applications every time we have to converse with others.

Reaching final judgment, undeniably translating application though being super machines are just a help but surely do not make men free from the practice of learning languages. Learning a foreign language has great significance, is my conclusion.

Public celebrations are held in many countries. Some people say that these celebrations are a waste of money and we should spend money on more important things. To what extent do you agree or disagree?

Public celebration means fairs and festivals which are often seen as a way to promote community spirit and bring people together. However, the cost of these celebrations can be exorbitant, and many argue that they are a waste of money as these significant funds could be better spent on other essential services. Their matter of concern may be genuine to some extent but importance of public celebrations cannot be overlooked too.

At the outset, it is argued that public celebration requires a giant sum of money to arrange big shows like on Republic Day every state spends lakh of rupees to showcase the progress and prosperity of their state in the form of a tableau, Diwali celebrations would remain incomplete until unless million of rupees are burnt off in the name of firework.

Similarly flaunting goes with other massive shows of national importance. But can such huge spending be justified when there are serious issues prevailing in the society like all people do not have access to education; good medical facilities, job opportunities and thousands of unfortunate mouths go unfed every day.

If people of a country are not in happy living circumstances, these mega shows are useless and sheer waste of money.

It is proposed that instead of putting money on temporary events,it is better to use the funds to improve infrastructure of a country and to better the lot of underprivileged folks.

Nevertheless, I personally have different perception like expenditure on programs of national importance must not be taken as superfluous expenditure. National events, whether it is a celebration of independence, a major sports tournament or a historic moment, are significant milestones for any country.

If these national celebrations are organized well, they are expected to provide a unique opportunity for citizens to come together and form a sense of unity and pride in their country. As such, it helps promote a sense of national identity and unity which is crucial for the long-term prosperity of any country.

One another fact is that this positive portrayal helps to enhance not only the country's reputation, encouraging foreign investment and tourism but helps countries develop economical trade and thus ensures prosperity for common public at large scale.

To sum up, the above mentioned fears regarding the expenditure seems very true since issues like poverty, unemployment etc. can be addressed with good finances only but at the same time celebration of events of national importance is surely not a waste of money as they being events of great national significance.

EASY TIPS
FOR
COMPLEX SENTENCES

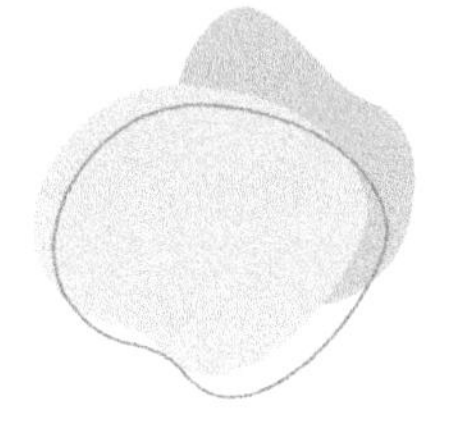

Use the 'ing' form to start sentences

Walking down the street provides good exercise.

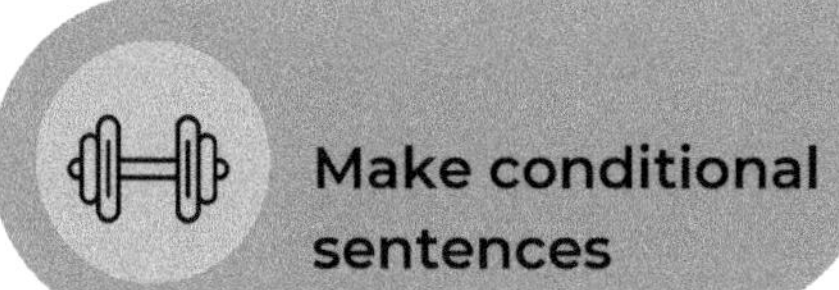

Make conditional sentences

Environmental conditions will not improve **until** people realize their responsibility towards nature.

Make Passive Sentences

New chapters have been introduced in new school curriculum.

Make use of question words

Cars **which** are auto-mated are also dangerous.

Make contrast

Some find cycling a good way of commuting **whereas** others see the negative side of it.

AMRITASHAAN

Preface

Discussion questions typically require an in-depth answer that takes into account all aspects of the debate concerning a research topic or argument.

There will be two opposing views and you will be asked to discuss both sides of the argument. You must demonstrate reasoning skills with this type of question, by using evidence to make a case for or against a research argument.

There are different types of topics which may be given to you, of which one is Discussion or Two-sided Essay. For this type of essay, you are expected to give arguments for both the sides and finally you will decide which side of arguments you are going to follow.

31

Some people say that the bicycles are a good, modern means of transportation. Other say riding a bicycle has clear disadvantages. Discuss both view points and give your own opinion.

Bicycle is one of the oldest mode of transportations which has always been in use though may be by a fewer people today. It is considered to be a wonderful mode of commuting whilst others find it imperative to highlight its negative repercussions. It is important to scan both the views to form some final view about this mode of transportation.

To start with, the cycle lovers find it good as it is very pocket friendly vehicle which can be afforded even by people with poor wages. Neither parking nor fuel consumption is another issue with this light mode of transportation. Riding down the city lanes on cycle is a great fun and those who know how to ride a cycle finds it comparatively easy to balance heavy vehicles too. In addition, time when environmental deterioration is a serious concern, the use of cycle is promoted as it being eco-friendly, hardly damages the environment.
To exemplify, the countries like Singapore where cycle is used by maximum people, enjoys fresh environment with no layers of black smoke as this machine does not add any pernicious elements in nature.

Furthermore, being in a sedentary life style, people find cycling to be the best way to work out. The physical exercise provided by it, is better than going to any gym for daily exercises.

However, it is not sunshine everywhere. The shady side makes the opponents dubious about the benefits of cycle. First, it is taken to be very unsafe vehicle. Their fear is genuine as they reckon that gone are the days when everyone was having cycle and people would have the routine to ride to their schools or workplaces. City lanes were safe as hardly any heavy vehicle was seen on the roads. Today when speedy heavy vehicles rush on the roads all the time, a cyclist finds it very hazardous to paddle around. Fatal accidents of cyclists further dishearten people and they avoid making use of it. Secondly, the greatest disadvantage is that it is not a vehicle for long distance because neither it can save people from rain and storm nor it can provide a luxurious ride to the commuters.

Generally speaking, looking at the both sunny and shady sides of it, I have reached to a conclusion that though there are many disconcerting issues with the use of cycle but still it is amazing mode of transportation as it is pocket-friendly, echo-friendly and a fun ride that also ensures good exercise to its user.

32

Some people say that advertising is extremely successful at persuading us to buy things. Other people think that advertising is so common that we no longer pay attention to it. Discuss both these views and give your own opinion.

Advertising is a powerful commercial tool used by companies to convince the buyer to buy the products they hype. A section of society acknowledges its tremendous success whereas others hold entirely different views that advertisements being very common are not attended well today. Scanning both the views will help me reach my perception.

To begin with, the supporter claim that the main reasons advertising is so successful is that they are present everywhere. We may open television, work at internet, access social media platform or go down the lane, the promotion clips will attract us and its repeated show eventually succeeds influencing the target clients. To exemplify, studies reveal that the products which are repeatedly advertised reaches their unexpected sale.

Admittedly, advertisements create a sense of need and often present products as necessities rather than luxuries, making one feel that life would be incomplete without it. For examples, mothers rush to buy energy drinks for their growing up kids as an ad has played on their mind that their child will grow tall, if energy drink is given to him at breakfast time.

Alternatively, many stand with the view that advertisements have lost their importance today. Modern buyers are prudent enough to understand the real objective of the advertisements. They know that it is a trap laid by the companies in which the benefits of a product are presented in an exaggerated form. Instead of depending on these hypes, they rather read the reviews before putting anything in their cart.
Importantly, people have become desensitized and numb to their messages and if they get irritated, pop ups are deleted, ads clips are skipped, newsletters are directed to spam mail and pamphlets find the place in the bins.

Finally, after analyzing the arguments of both the sides I came to conclusion that thought modern buyer is quite wise and understands the real motive of advertisements but nevertheless advertisements have their significance and to great extent they are successful as they make people buy the products they promote.

Some people believe that higher education should be funded by the government. Others, however, argue that it is the responsibility of individuals to fund their higher education. Discuss both views and give your opinion.

Entering college or university premises after attaining graduation in schooling has always been a dream of every student but cost of education reasonably remains a matter of concern which divides people in a debate like who should be the provider of funds for tertiary education, government or the funds be paid by individual himself. Scanning of both the views will help me reach my observation.

A group that stands in accord with the idea that higher education should be funded by the government opines that it is like an investment in the country's future. To explain it more clearly, education is fundamental to the economic growth and prosperity of a nation as with a high level of education, people are equipped with the knowledge and skills and an educated workforce is essential for a country's development. The most tangible paradigm is the input of taxes to government treasury by educated part of the society.

To move on, it is generally noticed that higher education remains a distant dream for those coming from poor financial background. Government funding will be a welcoming invitation to them to their dream institutions. Importantly, investing in higher education will prove a crucial tool to reduce crime rates, improve social well-being, and promote overall mental and physical health. Since education makes people more decent, they learn to communicate and solve problems that they encounter in their daily lives.

Another section of society proposes individuals to wear the onus of tertiary education by themselves as it is an investment in themselves which enables one to acquire skills and knowledge that make them more competitive in the job market. Higher education offers opportunities for career advancement and higher salaries and eventually ensures financial stability in life.

Secondly, Since every student wants to be in the study stream of his choice, bearing the expenditure of one's own education enables individuals to have control over their educational and career paths. Individuals can choose the course they want to study, the institution they want to attend, and the career path they intend to follow. Taking personal responsibility for funding one's higher education eliminates external factors such as government funding and scholarship programs which may limit the choices.

Finally, taking a look at both the aspects, I firmly opine that if governments takes the liability and ensures free higher education, it will not only open doors of education for people with monetary constraint but it will be an investment of government in itself only where skilled workers will provide strong economical structure to the state and bring prosperity and peace in the society.

34 **Some people think that it is important to use leisure time for activities that improve the mind, such as reading and doing word puzzles. Other people feel that it is important to rest the mind during leisure time. Discuss both views and give your opinion.**

Leisure hours are the most awaited time of a day but there is a contentious argument how to make use of this free time. Some individuals assert that spare time should be spent on some healthy indoor activities whereas others are inclined to the view that it is essential to rest without intentionally having any thoughts to recharge the mind. I am going to discuss both the views to reach my verdict.

To start with, leisure time is a precious time that can be used to enhance mental well being. Engaging in activities that stimulate the mind and also offers an opportunity to learn new skills, gain knowledge is recommended by some intellectuals. One way to use leisure time to improve the mind is by reading which enhances cognitive abilities and increases vocabulary besides It also offers an opportunity to gain knowledge about various topics of interest.

Adding to the argument, participating in mind games or puzzles tremendously benefits mental health as it improves memory retention, problem-solving, and critical thinking skills. To strengthen the view, the medical studies reveal that like any part of body, mind also needs good exercise to stay alive dynamically.

Turning the coin, the people who think differently advise to relax mind in free hours of the day and the reason is that in the current fast-paced world, where work pressure and stress levels are at an all-time high, it is more important to unwind and detach ourselves from our daily routine.

Our mind needs to be in a state where it could enjoy complete tranquility with no discursive thinking. Various studies have shown these practices can help reduce anxiety, improve concentration, and boost our mood. Taking time for self-care is essential to relaxation.

Finally, the complete discourse makes me believe that the different arguments have reasons. I think to some extent, it is a personal matter as some may be happy keeping mind engaged even during leisure time but for me allowing mind complete rest and a state where there is no thought, would be better option for me and it makes brain muscles relax and be ready for work again enthusiastically.

Understand the sentence structure

Participating in mind games or puzzles tremendously benefits mental health as it improves memory retention, problem-solving, and critical thinking skills.

35

Some believe that physical exercises should be included as a compulsory period in schools whereas some negates the idea by saying that schools are for academic studies only. What do you think is right?

There have been many heated discussions regarding the education pattern, specifically about including physical exercises in the school program of study. However some hold a view point that main objective of an institution is to prepare the students for their academic pursuits. Scanning both the views will help me frame my point of view.

To begin with, the advocate of inclusion of physical exercises in schools tend to believe that too much work for a long time lowers the efficiency of absorbing the knowledge whereas exercises will not only keep them more active and agile in their lessons but will also develop the culture of taking care of health right from the very beginning of life otherwise the young kids grow up with health issues like obesity and stress etc.

To add on, in the contemporary society, multi-task students are more acceptable than those who possess only bookish information. By participating in physical exercises, children not only keep themselves fit and healthy but also imbibe practical skills, such as interpersonal skills, the sense of healthy competition, the courage to overcome difficulties and how to face ups and downs etc. For example it is medically proven that regular physical exercises improve memory power and concentration, keep them motivated and teach the young minds how to fight stress etc which are the required nuts and bolts for their future life and career.

Alternatively, other section of society argues that educational centers should focus chiefly on the academic excellence of the students in order to impart formal extensive education. They feel that, in the end, the primary goal of education is to prepare students for the workforce and that those who excel academically will be better prepared for success in their future careers.

Ultimately, I reiterate, while academic studies are undoubtedly important, school curriculum should also have time for physical exercises. A balanced approach can help students thrive both in and out of the classroom. By providing a well-rounded education, we can ensure that students are not only prepared for their future careers, but also for healthy life as well.

Practice the art of paraphrasing as it will beautify your language.

36 Many governments think that economic progress is their most important goal. Some people, however, think that other types of progress are equally important for a country. Discuss both these views and give your own opinion.

Progress of a nation depends on the policies and programs of a country. There always remains a hot discussion on the topic where economical advancement is believed to be the sole aim by some whereas other intellectuals stress the need of development in other field too. After going through both the arguments, I will state my point of view.

Pondering over the first view, the ruling authorities take economic progress as their primary goal in order to increase in the standard of living for the citizens and overall prosperity of the country. Economic growth leads to an increase in gross income which translates to more investment in industrial sector, eventually leading to the elimination of poverty from the society and ensuring that everyone has everything for a good life.

Counting another fact, economically strong government provides robust foundation to a nation by erecting strong army which is always in form to face any natural disaster or foreign aggression. If a nation is monetary healthy, it is more likely to have respectable profile at international platform.

To prove it, the example of wealthy nation like America is there which rules the world in many ways.

Focusing on the other side of view, education is one another driving force behind a country's progress. A country can only reach its full potential if it invests in its education system. Education is not only important for an individual's personal growth but it also plays a significant role in a country's social stability and elite society contributes in the construction of society where there is peaceful environment with no crime rate.

Importantly, another argument is that health sector plays a critical role in the progress of any country. Health systems and services are critical in ensuring access to quality healthcare services, promoting life expectancy, reducing infant and child mortality, and improving the overall quality of life of the population. A healthy population is fundamental to a powerful nation.

To wrap up, I can say that indisputably well built economical country ensures prosperity for all but at the same time, development of education and health sector too needs to get prioritized as educated people will aid construction crime free society and sturdy health sector will keep the citizens safe from health issues.

SOME GOOD WORDS

INTIMIDATED FRIGHTENED	MONETARY FINANCIALLY	WEARISOME TEDIOUS
PHENOMENAL REMARKABLE	CONFRONTATION CONFLICT	INFLUX FLOW
INCLINATION TENDENCY	SAPIENT EDUCATED	GRAVE SERIOUS
VENERATION ADMIRATION	QUANDARY UNCERTAINTY	CONTENTIOUS DISAGREEABLE
REALIGNMENT REFORMATION	ABBREVIATE SHORTEN	UNRAVEL EXPLAIN

37 Some say that the standard of behaviour among children has worsened and that this is their parents' fault and others say that schools are to blame. Discuss both views and give your own opinion.

Deteriorating demeanor among modern children is a matter of debate as it is asserted by some that parents have the entire fault for their misconduct while others put all the blame on educational institutions. Through arguments from both the sides will help me reach my final judgment.

The case forwarded by first group of people is that parents carry the primary responsibility for their children's behavioral development and neglecting that responsibility can result in misconduct. Parents who do not teach their children basic principles like honesty, respect, and compassion set them up for misconduct. It is crucial to ensure that a child's environment is conducive to their growth and development to prevent them from indulging in any harmful misconduct.

To add on, the lack of moral guidance is a significant contributor to a child's behavioral misconduct, such as stealing or bullying. Therefore, parents are accountable as they fail to lay the right foundation. For example, If a child is exposed to harmful situations, it is their parents' responsibility to intervene, protect and guide them as any dereliction at their part may uphold child's misconduct.

Alternatively, the other argument is, the school environment greatly impacts the mental health, learning, and behavior of students. Due to the high workload, strict rules, and discipline, children feel stressed, anxious, and overwhelmed. The school's inability to address the needs of the students further exacerbates the problem.

Secondly, the school curriculum is often designed in a way that does not cater to every student's learning needs. Some students excel in conventional teaching methods, while others struggle. When students feel disconnected from their studies, they may become disengaged and start engaging in misconduct.

Admittedly, schools often fail to tackle bullying, which is a leading cause of misconduct among children. Bullying is a widespread problem that affects a large percentage of students. It can lead to low self-esteem, anxiety, and depression, which can manifest into misconduct.

Scanning both the views makes me analyze that if young adults exhibit impolite, insulting, rude and disrespectful behavior, both parents and their educational institutions can be held accountable for the same for all above discussed reasons. I can easily conclude with a suggestion that families and schools together should create a culture of accountability where students get best guidance and where their problems are dealt with nicely to help them behave appropriately.

38

Some people think that paying regular tax is enough to contribute to the society. Other argue that being a citizen one has more responsibility as well, to fulfill. What is your opinion ?

An amount of money that a government requires people to pay according to their income is known as tax. A section of people is happy by paying tax only and taking leave of their responsibilities towards society. While other argue that there are many other things that people are expected to realize as their liabilities towards the society they are living in. The controversy needs complete debate to reach the final point.

To begin with, the people who gives importance to paying regular tax hold an opinion that if people are sincere tax payer, they are honest contributor to the society because it is one of the most important duties of every citizen for the development of the country as it makes a government economically strong and government's treasury remains full of funds. Taxation is the primary source of revenue for the government and collected funds are utilized to provide essential services such as education, healthcare and infrastructure development etc. For example study reveals that states where people sincerely pay tax are generally more developed states as compared to other states.

Turning the other side of the page, the other brains believe that being a citizen everyone comes with a plethora of responsibilities towards the community they are living in. One of the most important is the obligation to contribute positively to society. If one lives in love and peace with his friends and folks, obeys the rules and laws of his country, his efforts are going to build a society worth living.

Secondly, as human beings, we have a moral obligation to help those less fortunate and to care for the environment. A good citizen donates time and money to charities, volunteers for community cleanups, and takes steps to reduce social imbalance in the society.

Hitting the last nail, I believe that though timely payment of taxes surely is conducive in the making of an economically strong society which enables its government to continue with the works of progress but at the same time it would be further favourable if citizens also take care of destitute and work for charities and make efforts to preserve nature. I would like to conclude that the list of society work is long and being good dwellers one should always stay positive to accept any responsibility they come across.

39

Some people say that fashion effects our life in a negative way. However others say that it has more positive effects on our life. Discuss both the views and give your opinion.

Fashion is a part of human culture that has been shaping the society in terms of their dressing sense, footwear, lifestyle, accessories etc. Some people find the aspect to be damaging and other see the brighter side of it. I need to scan both the views to reach some conclusion.

To start with, some critics unfairly target that fashion is always changing and people are willing to follow the latest trends to fit in with the crowd. However, the constant pursuit of fashion products has a negative impact on our lives as our finances can be affected detrimentally. People often spend large amounts of money on new clothes, shoes and accessories to stay up-to-date which can lead to financial instability.

Another charge on fashion is that it negatively impacts our body image and self-perception leading to unrealistic expectations. The constant demand to keep up with fashion trends means people often feel the need to be conventional to a certain body type, height or weight to fit in. This leads to people going to unhealthy lengths to attain the perfect fashion look or body image like, skipping meals or taking extreme weight loss measures.

The supporters of fashion see the rosy side of it and assert fashion helps us exude self-assurance and establishes our identity in social and professional settings as it boosts our self-esteem and confidence when we dress up in an outfit that we love and feel comfortable in. It automatically lifts our mood and makes us feel confident. As we step out into the world, we carry this positivity with us, which in turn influences our demeanor and interactions with others.

Secondly, fashion is celebrating diversity and inspiring people to feel comfortable in their own skin. Fashion shapes our perception of beauty and encourages us to embrace our unique features. It is not just about being skinny or having perfect skin but about appreciating and respecting our individuality. The fashion industry has started promoting diversity which is great news for people who may not fit the conventional beauty standards.

After having viewed perception of both the sides, I can conclude that there may be a few dark side of fashion but ultimately it is a wonderful culture by which we can express our individuality, connect with others, and shape the world around us. Surely, it is a wonderful aspect of human culture that deserves to be celebrated and explored.

40

There seem to be an increasing number of crimes committed each year. While some think the best way is to use the death penalty as a deterrent, many believe that other measures will be needed. Discuss both the views and give your opinion.

An alarming surge has been observed in the occurrence of illegal actions within our community as each year goes by. Hiking number of crimes make people believe that it is only death sentence which can check this problem while other find it important to think of other alternatives. My verdict requires to view both the arguments thoroughly.

The advocates of harsh punishment perceive that death penalty is an important aspect of justice. If a sinner inflicts harm on others, he is accountable for his misdeeds otherwise there will be no law and order in the society. The fear of death sentence will be a lesson for potential offenders and implementation of punishment will bring justice to the victim of crime.

The most tangible paradigm is the death sentence of rapists who were hanged till death and along with the victim's family the whole nation got a sense of justice.

In addition, criminals are the cancerous part of society and it is important to root them out. If they are allowed to grow, they are more like to spread poison in the society. Ending their life will not only keep the society safe but immoral activities will be checked remarkably.

The defenders on the contrary come up with different set of ideas and explore alternative measures of punishment. Like firstly, community service can be one of the most popular alternatives to death sentence. This involves offenders performing a particular form of service, as it forces offenders to become part of the community, thereby making them accountable for their actions.

Secondly, restorative justice is another alternative measure where the offender takes responsibility for his actions and makes amends for the harm caused to the victim or victim's family. This measure can allow him to reform himself and repairs the wounds given to the victim.

As a final point, unlawful activities make life insecure and unsafe which makes people believe that culprits, evil doers are rotten part of society and it is better to throw them away by taking their lives. Though logical thinkers have their own views but I believe that other alternatives should be taken into practice. Community service will help him become the part of society and restorative justice will allow him heal the wounds he had given to the society.

EASY TIPS
FOR
COMPLEX SENTENCES

Make Use of Connectors

To begin with, The most powerful argument in favour of it is that, Looking at it from different angle

Make Use of Time Linkers

When making plans for space exploration, we need to wear in mind the existing problems on the earth.

Use the 'ing' form to start sentences

Forgetting moral values of society will further lead to the deterioration of principles from the society.

Make conditional sentences

People will not follow rules unless they do not have fear of fine.

Show concession

Despite being an affluent nation, the grave health problems lie unattended.

AMRITASHAAN

Preface

Positive or Negative development questions typically presents a situation or a trend which can be good or bad. You are expected to choose between the two situations and take your stand and importantly need to make it very clear in the introduction.

You will explain your answer in body paragraphs.

This kind of question is quite simple because you are given a **development** and you have to decide whether that is positive or negative. There is nothing difficult about this. But it is advised to understand something deeper. Once you have chosen one option, do not talk about other side; try to justify your perspective. Your relevant example will help you write persuasively.

 In some countries, young people do not take care of their elderly relatives.Instead, they appoint trained professionals who take care of the elderly people. Is it a positive or a negative trend according to you?

Our parents or grandparents are the pillars of our families who need extra care in the stage of life. But in some parts of the world, the youth are not customary to look after their elderly parents rather as an alternative they hire trained professionals so that they could attend the elderly folk in the absence of their children. I believe it is a good decision at their part and surely an appreciating step.

At the outset, the reality of life is that in spite of having all the concern, it becomes troublesome for people to take care of their elderly parents properly with the responsibilities of bringing up children, running the household chores, managing office work. The life of modern youth is so professionally gripped that they hardly get family time and thus not to think that they would be sitting giving them message or making timetable for their daily tablets. The professionally trained people not only deal with their psychological and behavioral issues efficiently but keep them engaged in daily different activities for their happy routine. For example, even old people do not feel neglected or abandoned in the company of the care takers.

In addition, since, old age is a time of physical infirmities where the

the individuals in this stage often struggle to perform their daily tasks independently. It is advisable for them to receive assistance from professionally trained caregivers, especially when there is no one else at home to provide support. Proficient nurses oversee the daily dietary needs of individuals and ensure timely administration of medications. Their dedication to maintaining a well-organized life contributes to the overall health and well-being of the elderly, enabling them to lead a healthy lifestyle.

To conclude, in certain countries, young individuals opt not to personally care for their elderly family members, choosing instead to hire trained professionals. These caregivers address not only physical frailty but also psychological and behavioral concerns in the elderly, making professional assistance valuable during the challenges of old age. Thus hiring trained professionals to care for the elderly is a beneficial choice.

Responsibility - obligation
Nutritious - healthy
Positive - appreciating

42 **Film stars and celebrities often share their views on public matters that have little to do with their profession. Is this a positive or negative development?**

Film stars are some of the most influential and visible people in society who are idolized by millions of fans. In recent years, there has been a trend of famous people sharing their views on public matters, giving their opinions on everything from politics to social issues and most interestingly this hardly deals with their own profession. I personally believe that their engagement in public issue can be looked upon as a positive change.

To begin with, one of the benefits of big guns sharing their views on public matters is that it can raise awareness about important issues. Many times these renowned people of the society show their concern about the burning public issues and raise a strong voice in the public domain which makes their followers aware and make then ponder over the issue. This serves to create awareness and spark public discourse on issues that affect our planet.

To elaborate it further, famous people have a large following on social media and can reach a broad audience with their opinions. Many times main stream media ignores serious social issues but when film stars share their views on public matters, it draws media attention and amplifies the message which not only goes for public scrutiny but many times the problems reaches even to the deaf ears of the government. For example, when actress Emma Stone spoke out about the gender salary difference in Hollywood, it sparked a larger conversation about pay disparities in other industries as well.

Last not least, if these admired people talk about maintaining health or doing charity for the underprivileged people, a great number of fans can be found taking same action. Like Tiger Sharoff's comments on healthy lifestyle on social handles, motivated the youth to join gym and avoid taking drugs.

In conclusion, personal perceptions shared by big screen magnates on public matters is not only good for generating public awareness and making authorities hear the issues but it also helps to mobilize people towards taking action and creating change.

CELEBRITY : Big shot, Superstar, Personage, big gun, celeb, Big name, Renowned people, Public figure

WORK ON WORD POWER

43

The development of technology has resulted in more employees working from home. Is it a positive or negative development?

Modern technology is on its rampant wings and bringing incredible changes not only in our life style but also remodeling our professional working pattern. The latest vicissitude is the culture of working from home. I take it for acceptable change for the society as it brings many positive aspects with it.

To begin with, gone are the days when a person would get up early to get ready to reach his place of work and a little delay in reaching office might take him for explanation to his senior. The advent of technological devices and platforms like computer, internet, Google meet, Microsoft team, etc has unprecedentedly given the liberty to work from home. The most vivid positive change is that employees today save themselves from the hassle of daily commuting to workplace.

The new trend deserves all appraisal as remote workers can create their own schedules that accommodate their work and personal life. This freedom allows employees to work when they are most productive, leading to a more effective and efficient workflow. Moreover, with the absence of long commutes and other distractions typically found in the office, remote employees can dedicate more time and energy to their work, leading to better outcomes.

To add on, professional liabilities many times make a person neglect his family responsibilities as he hardly get any escape from his office work. Overtime jobs, long meeting, official get-together and presentations etc. keep people away from duties at home. Whereas working from home allows a person ample time to handle all fronts efficiently.

Last not least, there is win-win situation not only for employees but also for employers as remote work also breaks down geographical barriers and has enabled companies to hire top talent from anywhere in the world. Having a diverse team with different skill sets and backgrounds can enhance creativity and lead to improved productivity.

To sum up, working from home has come up as a new rising sun which is making working scenario easy for the employees and employers both. Where companies are getting enhanced quality work from best hired skilled labour from different parts of the world, the workers scheduling their working hours according to their ease and also giving quality time to their families.

44 **Nowadays, young people admire film stars and sport stars though they often do not set a good example. Do you think this is a positive or negative development?**

Film stars and sport starts are followed and idolized by millions of admirers of young generation. However presently it has been noticed that young folk admire even the actors and the players who do not even come up with positive aspects rather set shadowy unappreciable patterns in the society. I firmly believe that it is an adverse development for the community.

To raise a point, movie stars with negative role in movies can be violent, vulgar or display unacceptable social behavior. When people look up to these characters, they may be influenced in a negative way and make harmful or unethical decisions. For instance, a person who admires a film star who constantly smokes or drinks heavily, may start to take up these habits and not only harm their health but also set indecent standard in the society.

Additionally, negative role film stars may promote harmful stereotypes and beliefs. Like if a lead hero enjoys teasing female characters on the screen, the young folk is more like to go for eve-teasing. For example, films that promote misogyny and sexism will impact how people view women in their personal lives.

Similarly, the youth idolize their favorite players, follow them and try to adapt their behavior patterns. Unfortunately, when the players behave in an inappropriate manner, it negatively impacts the youth's overall development.

instead of exhibiting ideal behaviour in the play ground, some players use abusive language, exhibit disrespectful behavior, and make racist or sexist comments, all of which can be highly impressionable which not only hurts their well-being but also shapes admirers' mindset to think that such behavior is normal and acceptable.

On a final note, when youth observe their role models, who are the professional movie stars or players, who showcase wrong behavior, it not only negatively impact their performance but also retard the moral development of the youth in the society.

Plan your essay before you start writing and your every sentence should have some purpose to serve.

More and more people wear fashionable clothes. Is this positive or negative development?

Fashion has always been one of the most fascinating and exciting topics for people around the world and there is an interesting say about fashion ; Fashion is like eating, you should not stick with the same menu. Undeniable a section of society today has adopted to be trendy and stylish in their dressing sense. Being a supporter of fashion I see the positive side of it and take it as a good development.

First and foremost, dressing fashionably is an excellent way to boost one's overall happiness. When one feels good about their appearance, they are naturally happier and more content with themselves.
To make it more clear, when one looks good, he feels good. As human beings, we all have the desire to look and feel best and fashion can help us achieve this. A fashion-forward outfit can make an individual look attractive, confident, powerful, and ready to take on the world.

In addition, wearing fashionable dresses can also have a significant positive impact on an individual's social well-being. Fashionable outfits can help individuals stand out in a crowd and can also help break down social barriers. If one accepts the new trends of fashion world, they not only facilitate the society with newness but also make people experience the easiness of new dress which are believed to be more comfortable for causal and formal wear.

Moreover, wearing fashionable dresses allows individuals to express their unique sense of style and personality. Fashion provides an opportunity for individuals to experiment creatively, mixing and matching different pieces to create a look that is uniquely theirs.
This process of self-expression can be incredibly empowering, allowing individuals to embrace their individuality and celebrate their differences. It also allows individuals to show off their creativity and ingenuity, making them feel more proud of their fashion choices.

In the nutshell, wearing fashionable dresses is an incredibly positive development in today's society as it contributes cheerfully to an individual's self-esteem, social well-being, and overall happiness where individuals reflect their unique sense of creativity style and personality.

SOME GOOD WORDS

DUBIOUS DOUBTFUL	ACCORD AGREEMENT	ADHERE STICK FIRMLY
VOCATION JOB	MUNDANE ROUTINE	CONCISE SUMMARY
PAUCITY SCARCITY	ENDORSE SUPPORT	ADROIT SKILLFUL
VINDICATE JUSTIFY	ELUCIDATE EXEMPLIFY	BLATANT SHAMELESS
FACILITATE HELP	CIRCUMSPECT CAREFUL	AMELIORATE MAKE BETTER

46

In the world of the internet, people write product reviews of products and services. Do you think this is a positive or negative development?

Product evaluation is essential to the legitimacy of any e-commerce business. Review means to give analytical judgment on the quality of some product, service or an article etc. the trend of writing critical analysis for the products people buy and use has emerged as a common practice in the age when people have engaged in the world of internet. Though every coin has two sides but I would like to take it as a brilliant development and will prove it with my convincing arguments.

Firstly, writing review is like a right that a buyer has by which the manufacturers or service providers can be told about the quality of their products. Positive feedback not only boosts the sale of the product but also helps the company know the choice of the buyers. If the comments are negative, the service providers take steps to improve the quality and attend the grievances professionally.

Secondly, Reviews come as win-win situation for the sellers as one writes feedback only when one feels connected with product or company. It develops good understanding and relation between the two and company's authenticity is enhanced in the market. Since the reviews can be read by other potential buyers, the sellers have not to go for mouth to mouth promotion of the product. The testimonials establish the credibility of the businesses. For instance, market reports reveal that the products with maximum feedback further get remarkable hike in its sale.

Thirdly, testing and trying products is not something that a modern customer wastes his time in. Having being an aware buyer, he also depends on reviews before he puts any product in his cart. As it provides an overall understanding of what the product is, how it works, and whether it is worth buying or not. By reading others' reviews, new customers can avoid making mistakes and choose products that align with their needs. The testimonials become the guidelines for the buyers and influence their decision to a great extent.

In conclusion, writing reviews is a positive development as it helps new customers to make better choices by reading reliable reviews. Businesses, on the other hand, can use reviews to discover areas for improvement to further strengthen their reliability in the market.

47

In many countries around the world, young people decide to leave their parents' home once they finish school. They start living on their own or sharing a home with friends. Is this a positive or a negative development? Give reasons for your answers and include relevant examples.

Family culture in our society has seen great changes in the recent past and one of them is a trend of living independently or with friends on sharing basis which is preferred by young generation as soon as they complete their schooling. Living independently or with fellow mates both can be looked upon as an acceptable change and ensuing perspectives will make my perception clear.

To start with, I am likely to believe that life away from family at a very young age itself is an educational journey as a child learns to grow independent. Since parents are not around, one becomes responsible for his daily chores and does not look upon others to come and assist him. Rather he plans the things in advance to save himself from any type of mismanagement and inconvenience.

To add on, although they are not very mature at this stage of life but when they take their decisions themselves, they get an insight to understand what is right or what is wrong. To make it more clear, a young child himself takes decisions regarding his study time, friend circle, eating habit and money management etc. and eventually this decision taking quality helps him grow confidently in life. Thus going away from family is not a bad deal for him in terms of his personal growth.

Digging out more benefits, sharing accommodation with peers is another way to see the real spectrum of life. Family is the whole world for a child where he is in the safest zone of life. But practical life exists beyond one's own family where one needs to come in contact with people of different nature and temperament. Living with friends makes him more cooperative, humble, flexible, helpful, understanding and gives him a mindset where one learns to come out of his false prejudices. Besides this living with friends can offer opportunities for socializing and entertainment which can promote mental and emotional well-being.

To conclude, after schooling, the above mentioned trends can be taken as good change because it not only prepares the young heart to be ready to grow self reliant but also fill them with good social qualities. In the circle of friends one cheerfully continues the next phase of life.

48

Some people think that internet will replace traditional books in future. Do you believe this would be positive or a negative development?

The rise of technology has dramatically transformed our world, making everything more convenient and for book lovers, eBooks have been introduced as the new and improved way of reading books. Although eBooks have their benefits, they also come with an array of negative consequences, leading me to argue that replacement of traditional books will be a nocent adjustment.

The first thought that disturbs the mind is that the internet provides a screen to read which does not offer the same sensory experience as traditional books. The nostalgic aroma, the inviting cover pages, the touch of a book in its physical form, the colorful pictures, beautiful fonts create an experience that the internet will never match.

To make it more clear, taking books with beautiful covers and creamy papers in hands or showcasing them on study rack is something that an avid lover of books will have to sacrifice with this prejudicial change. One would never enjoy the exuberant experience of keeping flowers in the pages of the books and enjoy its fragrance while reading the favourite pages.

Second, if traditional books are replaced it would spoil the relation between the reader and the book because online content is often ephemeral while traditional books is designed to last for generations. A reader reads the book and develops an unflinching trust whereas materials online keeps upgrading leaving a reader in a dubious state of mind.

Third, the convenience of eBooks has led many to believe that they are the best form of reading, ultimately leading to a decline in physical book sales. With less demand for print books, there will be fewer physical bookstores, it will seriously result in the less exposure to literature. Inspite of accessibility to ocean of ebooks, people may lose interest in reading as physical appearance of books itself is quite inviting.

Last not least, It is also interesting to note that physical books do not have a negative effect on one's health as opposed to eBooks. So another negative change that can result from eBooks is the potential harm to one's health. The blue light that emits from electronic devices can cause eye strain, headaches and disrupt sleep.

In conclusion, the idea of reading from an eBook may seem appealing but the negative consequences are worth considering.

49

Nowadays sport is becoming a business and more in more professional and pick companies are getting involved in sporting events. Do you think it is a positive or negative development?

Sports events which are an integral part of society are being adopted by different professionals. The sponsorship gives a face lift to the sport industry and proves a boon for both the players as well as for the investors and it certainly can be taken as a fresh change healthy for society in many ways.

To start, sponsorship is like an invitation to the youth to take sports as their profession because it brings financial gains in terms of high salaries, other privileges and extra bonus at their outstanding performance. Money injected into the industry makes the youth see their bright future in sports industry which otherwise may not be a tempting zone for them.

In addition, sport events desperately need financial support. If there is a good flow of funding, the players are more likely to get the best resources for practice. It also allows them access to high-quality equipment, training facilities, good diet and specialist coaching that may not accessible otherwise. The players enjoy better exposure, more chances of participation, an opportunity to showcase their talents on a national or international stage.

Counting another positive aspect, it is a win-win situation for the sponsors too who by taking hold of the events get accessibility to the stadiums, where they easily advertise their products and create a buzz. Huge banners, bill-boards are fixed in the event grounds that catch the attention of millions of people. For example, the Pepsi, the Coca cola soft drink brands become a house-hold names during cricket tournaments.

Last not least, funding of sport not only ensures the dominance of the brand presence in the market but also endorses the brands by creating a large customer base in the market which eventually gets them enlisted as the consumers' preferred brand escalating the sale of their products.

In conclusion, it is evident that sport sponsored by corporate world is a positive development and brings win-win situation for the sportsmen who see their future career in the stream and get handsomely paid and at the same time helps the investors to reach their potential clients easily with extraordinary sale of their products.

50

In recent years, many small local shops have closed because customers travel to large shopping centers or malls to do their shipping. Is this a positive or a negative development?

There has been a rapid growth in the number of malls in major cities around the world and they have become a popular destination for shoppers. However, the opening of malls is a feeble spin for local markets.

To start with the first reason, survival of local business in the scenario where there are air conditioned malls around has become incredibly challenging. Malls which are more than just shopping centers; they offer entertainment, restaurants and other fun activities attract flock of people and this has led to the decline of crowd to small shops. The shopkeepers are facing a situation like getting unemployed.

To add on, the local sellers earn their livelihood by selling their local products in which farmers bring the production of their fields, many artisans sell the products of art and craft of traditional value. Even small vendors earn good if the market places get good customers there. For example, if market has great hustle-bustle, even a juggler will go happy to home by earning respectable amount by his monkey's show.

Notably, another fact which cannot be ignored is that it can lead to a decline in a community's culture and identity. Local markets are the places which buzz with different types of activities. A poor little girl can be found selling balloons and toys and a beggar would be there to beg for a few alms. People from different economical status visit to have recreation round of the places.

Without these small markets, people might lose this culture and touch with their heritage and the unique products that define their community.

Last not least, malls can lead to a more superficial culture. Malls offer a lot of materialistic distractions that can take people's attention away from social and cultural experiences. This can be a negative aspect of living in a mall-driven society.

In conclusion, the opening of malls is an infirm advancement for the local market as it is damaging to local products, market, shopkeepers and to community culture.

Relative clause – The people who are concerned about their society, need reorganization for their contribution.

Preface

IELTS problem solution essays deal with the questions in which you are given a situation and you are asked to talk about the problems the situation may create and you are also expected to give some suggestions how to solve them. The way they are worded can vary hugely which can make it difficult to understand how you should answer the question. The three essay types are:

· **Problem and solution**
· **Cause and solution**
· **Just the solution**

They are the most challenging essay type for many people because its questions can be worded in many different ways. Like;

- **What are the reasons for this and how can the situation be improved?**
- **What issues does this cause and how can they be addressed?**
- **What measures could be taken to prevent this?**

It will not take you much time, planning this type of question. You just need to think of two or three possible reasons for the situation and have to suggest the ways to handle them. You will be able to write well linked essay.

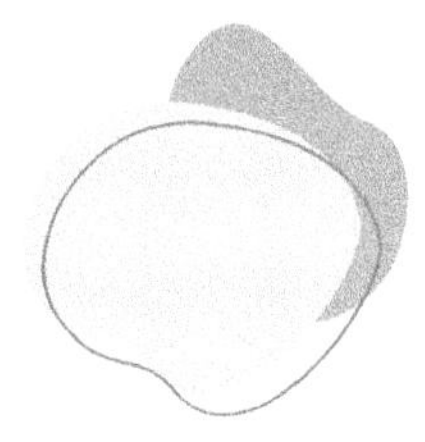

EASY TIPS
FOR
COMPLEX SENTENCES

Make conditional sentences

If you set your mind to a goal, you'll eventually achieve it.

Make Use of Time Linkers

As social media is there, people are losing contact face to face.

Make Passive Sentences

Traditional values **have been forgotten** today under the dominance of western culture.

Use the 'ing' form to start sentences

Working from home allows people to have time for their families too.

Make Contrast

Elderly folk enjoys great experience of life **whereas** the young generation has yet to know the realities.

AMRITASHAAN

51

The noise level around us is constantly increasing and affecting the quality of our lives. What causes the noise? What should be done about it?

Today, man is living amongst deafening noises which are not only on constant hike but also badly affecting the quality of life. It is essential to understand the potential reasons for increasing noise and some preventive measures are need to be taken as the situation still is not out of gear.

To begin with, urbanization refers to the growth of cities and their surrounding areas which often results in the rise of noise levels. As cities become bigger, there is an increase in traffic, construction, and the number of people living in close proximity. The blowing of traffic horns, rattling sound of running machines, deafening sound produced by generators or loud speakers are depriving the cities of serene atmosphere. These activities lead to more noise, thereby impacting the quality of life in urban areas.

Going on, technological advancements also play a major role in escalating noise levels. With the proliferation of advanced technologies, people often use electronic devices at high volumes. Many individuals have developed a culture of loud music which impacts the noise levels in society. Even in residential areas, people indulge in activities that generate noise, such as loud parties and music.

51

For example, medical sciences reveals that today more and more people are facing hearing problem not because they are growing old but because they are living in the maddening sound of the cities.

It is essential that people should understand these reasons and take responsibility to reduce noise pollution. First of all, urbanization now needs a check as no development is acceptable at the threat of human existence.
Secondly, means of transportation should be changed. Use of bicycle and electric operated vehicles instead of cars, trucks, buses etc. can be possible alternative.
Importantly, noisy leisure activities should be avoided by individuals and government must ensure that every industry has its sound proof systems. Insulated homes with noise controlling material will be a remedy for people surrounded with deafening noise.

Putting all in the nutshell, high level of noise is a matter of deep concern and urbanization and human activities are the root cause of it. The issue needs immediate attention and if above said measures are taken into consideration, the amplifying noise level can be controlled and peaceful environment can be restored.

52 **Many employers find that their new employees lack sufficient interpersonal skills such as lack of ability to work with colleagues as a team. What are the causes? Can you suggest some possible solutions?**

It is necessary to work effectively with colleagues as a team in order to succeed in any workplace. However, there are instances where an individual may lack the ability to work cohesively with others. There are a range of causes of this issue. However some solutions can certainly be proposed to ensure harmonious working environment.

Taking the first possible reason, students in their academic institutions are encouraged to achieve personal excellence in exams instead of guiding for collective aim to become supportive team players. Education system forces them to focus on personal gain and achievements and to defeat others instead to taking steps together towards the fixed target. Such a selfish temperament leads to toxic working culture.

Secondly, personality clashes are perhaps one of the most common reasons why individuals struggle to work well as a team. Everyone has their own set of personality traits leading to misunderstandings and conflicts. For instance, someone who is naturally introverted and quiet may find it difficult to work with someone who is outgoing and assertive.

52

Finally, If individuals are not willing to be flexible and adapt to different work styles, it can result in tension and conflict and will hardly allow people to enjoy cool working state of affairs together.

It is important to find solutions to address the lack of ability to work with colleagues as a team. One solution is to initiate team-building activities at school level to instill the qualities of working together in young minds. Further, if misunderstandings and miscommunications are hindering teamwork, it is important to establish effective communication channels. Encouraging regular, open communication between team members can help ensure that everyone is on the same page and everyone feels heard and understood. Lastly, assigning roles and responsibilities where all team members develop respect and understanding for each other can help promote collaboration.

Overall, there are several causes of a lack of ability to work with colleagues as a team, including personality clashes, communication barriers and differing work styles. However, above mentioned proposals can be beneficial to work proactively to establish a positive working environment.

53

People's lives are becoming increasingly stressful nowadays and there are many reasons behind this. In your opinion what are the reasons behind this? What can be done to solve this problem?

Stress is a common feeling experienced by individuals across all walks of life. There are various reasons that contribute to stress, ranging from personal and familial to professional and societal. Some judicious plans can help mitigate the acute affects of anxiety.

One of the most common reasons behind stress is work-related pressure. As life has become increasingly fast-paced and competitive, individuals must meet high expectations, work long hours, and face tight deadlines. The failure to do so can result in anxiety, restlessness, and burnout.

Additionally, due to the constant exposure the social media platforms, people are becoming increasingly concerned about fitting societal standards of beauty, lifestyle, and success. This perfect life image that others project makes people feel like they are not doing enough or are inadequate, which draws negative thoughts and emotions, ultimately leading to an increased sense of dissatisfaction.

Digging out another cause, personal relationships, especially familial, can cause substantial amounts of stress. Unresolved conflicts, growing distance, failing communication and a multitude of other reasons can trigger feelings of anxiety, helplessness, or frustration.

Importantly, financial problems are also a significant cause of stress. In today's world, financial stability is essential for a good quality of life whereas issues such as debt, unexpected expenses, or job loss can all increase stress levels.

It is important to recognize and address the sources of stress in one's life to avoid grave consequences on the body and mind. While it is easier said than done, finding a healthy balance between work and personal life, staying connected with loved ones, taking care of mental and physical health and setting realistic expectations are essential to lead a stress-free life.

In conclusion, strain is a natural part of life that affects us all in different ways. It is essential to identify the source of stress and take steps to manage it effectively as by this only we can improve our quality of life, cerebral health, and overall well-being.

Present your opinion and support it throughout the whole essay

EASY TIPS FOR COMPLEX SENTENCES

Show purpose

Making use of public transport is good as **by doing this** crowd of vehicles can be reduced

Make Use of Time Linkers

When making plans for space exploration, we need to wear in mind the existing problems on the earth.

Time linker

Whenever people access internet, they learn to use technology

Make conditional sentences

If children take fast food, they put on weight.

Show confession

In spite of being aware of the health issues, people hardly avoid junk food.

AMRITASHAAN

54

Nowadays people use bicycles less as a form of transport. Why is the case? What can we do to encourage people to use bicycles more?

Gone are the days when getting a bicycle had been a dream of every young child and would enjoy riding it as a daily mode of transportation. Apparently, in recent years, there has been a decline in the use of bicycles. This trend can be attributed to a number of factors. The essay will also ponder over the possible preparation to encourage people to make use of this wonderful means of commuting.

The most perceptible reason is the introduction of newer and more sophisticated modes of transportation, such as electric cars or public transport options which appeal to people in terms of time saving and comfort they provide. If one gets better option as per the changing needs of time, one cannot be expected to stay with obsolete trends thus decline in popularity of cycling is end result.

Additionally, lack of proper cycling infrastructure can be a major deterrent for many who seek comfort in more modern or efficient modes of transport. Cyclists have to compete with cars, buses, and pedestrians on narrow roads or sidewalks that are unevenly paved. Many are afraid to cycle because they believe it is too dangerous. Many accidents have caused unnecessary injuries or fatalities.

54

Talking about the other part of question, the first step to encourage the use of bicycles is to improve infrastructure. This includes creating safe and accessible bike lanes and paths.

Additionally, local governments offering incentives is another strategy for encouraging the use of bicycles. By recognizing and rewarding those who choose to cycle, more people will be motivated to adopt the behavior. Heavy taxes on the use of other vehicles can also divert people towards the use of cycle.

Finally, promoting a culture of cycling can be a powerful tool in encouraging its use. This can include organizing local cycling events and creating social groups for cyclists to connect and share stories and experiences. By normalizing cycling as a fun and healthy form of transportation, more people will be likely to adopt it as a regular part of their lives.

In conclusion, the popularity of using cycle is on refuse for many reasons but its use should surely be encouraged. By taking all required steps, we can create a world where cycling will be a normal and accessible form of transportation that will benefit both individuals and the environment.

55

The world natural resources are consumed at an ever-increased rate. What are the dangers of this situation? What should we do?

The consumption of global natural resources at an alarming rate is a disconcerting issue as there are some impending dangers associated with it. The essay aims to ponder over the expected threats along with some possible steps to tackle the situation.

To start with, though natural resources are for the use of all living being on the planet but overconsumption of it by humans is leading to depletion of these blessings. It is genuinely feared that future generation will crave for fresh air, clean environment and potable water. The most terrible situation which can be exemplified is the fear of the intellectuals of the world that the third world war will not be for earthly possessions but for survival.

To add on, since natural resources are non-renewable, they will become extinct one day. In absence of natural resources, man will enter a dark phase of life where he will have to struggle just for their existence. Though there will be ways but not the resources to make use of them. Industries will come to a halt, lack of production will create scarcity of everything leading to starvation and hunger in the world. Unbalancing in ecosystem will further degenerate the quality of life.

However, the situation is still not out of gear as with a few measures situation can be handled. Firstly, prudence use of gift of natures is the direst requisite of the hour. People need to understand that every leaf of a tree and every single drop of water matters today. Secondly, methods should be invented to make use of fewer resources, but for high density of population. Last not least, if more and more areas are conserved as forest reserves, a certain proportion of nature can be saved as a stimulant for new growth.

After analyzing the whole situation, it is easy to conclude the excessive utilization of nature is inviting a doom's day for the planet. Nevertheless with a little discretion, the situation can be handled.

Make sure your ideas are directly related to the question and Use ideas and examples that you are Make sure your ideas are directly related to the question and Use ideas and examples that you are familiar with.

56

Shopping has become a new favourite pastime for the younger generation. Why is this the case? Should we encourage them to develop other hobbies too?

Acceptably shopping has become an increasingly popular pastime among the youth. In this essay, I will explore why shopping has become a go-to hobby for many young people and will it be good if they are advised to adopt passion for some other free time activities too.

Firstly, shopping is an activity that the more you do, the more you go crazy for it as it itself is a delightful activity which provides a sense of instant gratification.
To make it more clear, it is believed to be a human tendency to visit market places or in the present time browse online stores to select and buy different type of things to pamper oneself with new collection of things.

Secondly, in a world, where trends are constantly evolving, shopping provides a way for young people to stay on top of the latest trends and be in the loop. They stay up-to-date with the latest styles, gadgets, and must-have items and believe that visiting markets is the only way for them to know what is there in vogue today.

The other validate reason can be, shopping is a stress buster activity for many of them which also allows them time for socializing. Visiting market places with families and friends not only works as fun activity but browsing through stores, trying on clothes and giving advice to each other can be a source of great fun and happiness for many young people.

Although shopping brings all excitement for the young generation but guiding them for other pastime activities can also be an essential intellectual dose for them. Like instead of carrying shopping bag if they play outdoor games, they are more likely to have fun besides good health. Getting relief from daily stress and socializing are other benefits they can get, provided that they are with their mates.

In addition, by reading good books, one gets to know the principles, ideology and thoughts of great men which eventually helps him develop his insight, makes him more knowledgeable and guides him in the dark phase of life.

To sum up, besides reaping the benefits of shopping, the young generation needs to turn a page to check some other activities too to further improve their living style.

SOME GOOD WORDS

PERCEPTIBLY	PURPOSELY	PREFERABLY
LAVISHLY	LIKELY	LEISURELY
OBLIVIOUSLY	OPENLY	OBJECTIVELY
JUDICIOUSLY	INCESSANTLY	INDIFFERENTLY
HOPEFULLY	HURRIEDLY	FORMIDABLY

MAKE GOOD USE OF ADVERS TO SCORE HIGH BANDS

Today, many big cities in the world are increasing in size. What are the problems associated with it? What are the solutions to these problems?

Cities are the heart of modern civilization and serve as the backbone of any country. Over the years, world population has multiplied rapidly, paving the way for the growth of urbanization. The essay is going to focus on the serious predicaments associated with the growth and some possible cures of the issue.

One of the most significant problems associated with enlarging cities is congestion. As a crowd of people flock to cities which inevitably leads to traffic jams with further related issues like, wastage of time, damaging the air quality and also affecting service delivery etc. For example, many times ambulance gets struck in heavy traffic and fails to drop the emergency patient to medical centre in time.

One more barrier associated with enlarging cities is deteriorating quality of air and water leading to the deterioration of healthy living environment. The people in mega cities hardly get a chance to see blue sky as layers of black smoke keep covering the sky most of the time. Wearing masks is a compulsion for them. Water pollution is also an everyday issue. The rapid urbanization of areas without proper resources, such as sanitation system often leads to the contamination of drinking water sources.

Taking about the remedies to repair the wound, first of all, construction of new roads can help to alleviate the situation. Since big cities get hundred of vehicles on the roads, if there are good network of roads, sideways, flyovers, footpaths etc. the traffic will remain moving.

To add on, for the improvement of air quality, work can be done to enhance greenery in the cities. Big campaigns of tree plantation will surely help to observe the impurities of the environment and make the air fresh.
Finally to overcome the problem of fresh water scarcity, the installation of more and more fresh water plants is needed.

To conclude, global growth of population is a matter of deep concern as it is causing the problem of congestion making urban people face the challenges of traffic jams, poor air and water quality etc. All the major roadblocks can be uprooted if above mentioned proposals are taken into consideration.

Never Over Generalize.

58

Nowadays the crime rate is increasing, especially among teenagers. What are the reasons behind it? How can we reverse this trend?

The most disconcerting fact commonly noticed today about the adolescents is their increasing tendency of involving in crime. Some most common factors of life can be held responsible for it which will be discussed in ensuing paragraphs along with some proposed efforts to reverse the trend.

To begin with, there is a well known fact that kids learn from the environment that live in. Inspite of having all comforts, if they are exposed to domestic violence, they are more like to grow aggressive, arrogant and unfeeling in their life. They are not expected imbibe the virtues of compassion, care and concern for others and always are more prone to slip in the world of sins.

To add on, having being in the company of friends who are unethical, immoral and hostile in their behavior, who are badly involved in drinking and smoking also drag the youth to the way which ends up in the lane of crime.
Sometime the problem of unemployment or high status life of other people make them feel depressed and they jump in offences like stealing, pick pocketing, robbing etc. to fulfill their unfulfilled dreams.

58

Moving no, an amount of youth with poor educational background always remain perturbed with a thought that they would never get a high profile job. They look for short cuts as they want to gain everything overnight. The world of crime welcomes such people of the present generation.

Talking about how to channelize the uncontrolled energy of the youth, the best solution is that the parents need to understand their moral duty towards their kids and have to groom them up with the virtues like patience, empathy, forgiveness, compliance and importantly desire to work hard for success.

Secondly, educational structure needs to revise the present requirements of the youth and inscribe a new curriculum which prepares the youth to earn handsomely with their skills, knowledge and information.

To sum up, the serious rise of juvenile crime is a result of some common reasons which can be put on the pin point. Reversal of trend also requires judicious steps and efforts from parents and teaching institutions.

People are living in a 'throwaway society', using things for a short time and then throwing them away. What are the causes of this? What problems does it lead to?

A throw-away society is an affluent society with throwaway mentality where materials that still could be used are thrown in the bins. There are many reasons of the trend of 'use and throw' approach. The repercussions, it is leading to are also worth considering.

Picking up the first reason, for many companies, manufactured products are only profitable if they are produced in large quantities and as cheaply as possible. Cheaper production generates a lower durability of goods that is why many goods like containers, bags, bottles, footwear, dresses etc for example, are used for short time as they are not made to last long and thrown away quickly.

Moving on, we humans strive for variety and get fed up with same styles. New trends, designs and developments serve this desire with countless and preferably inexpensive products. These short lived cheap goods and new trends stay hardly for a week intervals and then go out of sight and our accessories related with, find their place in the bins.

The most prominent visible reason is in particular, technical devices such as smart phones, computers and household appliances are nowadays built in such a way that users can have them repaired only at extremely high cost. Ultimately, the expensive repair than buying new, creates waste more rapidly.

Focusing on the consequences, the throwaway society shows its ugly side above all in the form of the garbage in the environment which not only spoil the beauty of towns and cities but also become the breeding place of insects threatening the outbreak of any viral disease.

Secondly, the fertile power of the land is spoiled by the disposals. Plastic, for example, is not biodegradable and basically stays in nature forever. Last not least, new products need more and more raw material which in turn depletes nature of its natural resources.

To encapsulate, the emergence of throwaway society is a product of many reasons like cheap production, craze for new fashions, high repair maintenance cost etc. The results are more upsetting as it is a direct threat to nature, making cities look ugly, inviting viruses, extraction of natural resources and making the soil barren.

You can divide your ideas while writing essay in different body paragraphs.

An increasing number of advertisements on TV aim at children. What are the effects of television advertising? Should television advertising be controlled?

Advertisements are the commercial strategy adopted by different companies to attract their potential clients. They are everywhere and importantly on television where children are exposed to them every day. It affects the children in many ways and thus they are required to be under check.

To start with, the most serious effect is that advertisements can promote unhealthy eating habits among children. For example, advertisements for fast food show children happily eating burgers, fries and ice creams. Inspite of being aware of unhealthy side of the junk products, the commercials capture young minds and make them take what kids eat in hypes.

In addition, blatant show of cigarettes, alcohol and other harmful substances are quite common on the screens and these matters are exposed to the kids daily and very early in their life. Young folk being influenced get engaged in risky behaviors, taking it if smoking or drinking is a normal part of growing up.

Lastly, glittery world of advertisements bring a trail of toys, candies, foot-wears, dresses etc. and children feel like tasting

60

and trying everything which creates financial stress for families that may not be able to afford such luxuries and disappointment for the children if they do not get the things they want.

Since there is over dose of hypes these days first and foremost it is necessary to control them as they are very distracting. Television is for entertainment but commercial breaks every few minutes are incredibly frustrating as they disrupt the flow of the show.

Controlling television ads is essential due to their adverse effects on children, as they often promote products that are not only harmful but also misleading and deceptive. This poses a risk as children may struggle to distinguish between reality and fiction.

To conclude, increasing number of advertisements targets the youngest audience and promotes unhealthy behaviors, unhealthy products, and negative image as well as distracts children from important aspects of their lives. For all these concerning effects it is believed to be kept under proper control.

> **Always read the question carefully and decide how many parts are in it. Write more than 250 words**

EASY TIPS
FOR
COMPLEX SENTENCES

Make conditional sentences

If rules are made strict, the situation will improve.

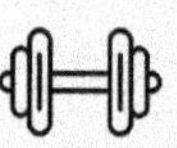
Make Use of Time Linkers

While buying things online, people ignorantly save their PIN numbers and face issues later.

Make Passive Sentences

Fast food **should be avoided** by people to enjoy a healthy life style.

Use the 'ing' form to start sentences

Guiding youth may seem difficult but fact is that they are still innocent and depend on their elders for important decisions.

Make Contrast

Old education system is producing excellent brains. New system **however** is still the need.

AMRITASHAAN

Preface

This is one another type of question of typical situation or a trend. You are asked to talk about the reasons of the situation and your another task is to give your opinion whether it is positive or negative change.

You can develop your essay by stating two or more reasons and then can explain what ever stand you take in terms of positive or negative change.

This may seem to be a little challenging task but there is nothing difficult about this. You are advised to give genuine reasons and try to justify your perspective for positive or negative change. Remember again you have to support one of the two choices.

The model answers to such type of questions will help you understand the structure better.

 Nowadays many people want to buy famous brands of clothes, cars and other items. What are the reasons for this? Do you think it is a positive or negative development?

Brand consciousness, a prominent characteristic of contemporary society, has led many individuals to invest substantially in maintaining an opulent lifestyle. This phenomenon is driven by several factors, and I am inclined to believe that this societal shift holds promising prospects.

Delving into the underlying causes, buying capacity of modern educated people has made everyone tag conscious. They are earning handsomely and plan to keep the best quality things with them.

Secondly, e-commerce can be held as another igniting element which has made all national and international brands accessible to everyone. Gone are the days when people were not aware of quality products, today they know the real worth of branded products which are believed to be durable and of high quality and the buyers happily open their credit cards for such shopping and e-gate enables them to put the things in their carts.

Lastly, the prevalent status consciousness in society contributes significantly to this trend. Branded products, perceived as symbols of enhanced reputation, offer not only prestige but also reliable quality and safety guarantees. Consequently, individuals are more inclined to purchase branded shoes, clothing, automobiles, and other items that signify both status and quality.

61

There is no doubt that brands are in vogue and it is a wonderful transition for the society. Like, the modern youth has turned out to be very ambitious who feel like working more hard provided that he earns good in order to spend lavishly on all classy products to have sophisticated life style.

Secondly, brands have given rise to healthy competition among different companies which are now in the race of bringing the best products in the market and also at competitive price.

Ultimately, products from reputable brands, known for their enduring quality, contribute to environmental friendliness by preventing a daily surge in waste and posing no threat to nature.

Completing the task, the use of brands is the culture of present society and should be taken as dynamic change because people try to earn good to get tagged products; companies bring quality products which last long and environment too remains intact.

Use punctuation to make your writing comprehensible.

Modern cultures around the world have become similar when compared to the past. What are the reasons? Is it a positive or negative development?

In the age of globalization, the exchange of ideas has led to a blending of cultures, resulting in many similarities between people from different parts of the world. There are some reasons behind the new change and the change is a shift towars positive direction.

One of the primary ways in which modern cultures have become alike is through movies, television shows and music from around the world that is all ubiquitous. Since core themes and values of these shows remain the same, people in different countries easily relate to the same cultural touchstones.

The spread of consumerism is another factor that has contributed to the connection of modern cultures. With the rise of global trade, people around the world now have access to the same goods and services. The most tangible paradigm is, from fast food to fashion, people from different parts of the world often consume the same products.

Continuing, the ease of travel has also played a role in the homogenization of cultures around the world. Business travel, tourism, and immigration have all enabled people to experience new cultures firsthand.

62

Homogenization of cultures can be seen as positive aspect of modern society as it brings the people of world community together. Instead of wearing any type of prejudices against other cultures, people learn about each other's beliefs, values, and way of life and thus leading a greater understanding and appreciation of diverse practices.

Additionally, when diverse cultures engage with each other, there is an exchange of ideas, and they are more inclined to adopt mutually beneficial practices. For example, the Japanese approach to medicine is now widely implemented across various regions globally. Lastly, the joyous acceptance of all cultures serves as a powerful catalyst, nurturing a world characterized by enduring peace and harmonious coexistence.

In conclusion, modern cultures around the world have become similar due to a variety of factors and it has proved as an excellent change because people across the globe are reaping benefits of it, adopting it as per their need, showing appreciation for diversities and with healthy acceptance of all they are constructing a peaceful society.

Words that are old-fashioned and not used in everyday speech should not be used.

63

Some young people are leaving the countryside to live in cities and towns, leaving only old people in the countryside. Why do you think is this? Do you think this is a positive or negative development?

Migration of the youth to cities and towns is a common visible trend that has been in practice for a few decades. The essay is going to probe in to the reasons and reach the conclusion whether the change is good or bad.

To begin, the most pressing reason is the countryside youth today is educated, enlightened and aware of great development going on around the world. He believes that if he moves to mega cities only then he can enjoy the benefits of technically growing world whereas remote areas will retard his personal growth.

To add on, urban areas provide vast scope for employment in industries, trade, transport and services. On the contrary, the agricultural base of rural areas does not provide employment to all the people living there. To make it more clear, even the small-scale and cottage industries of the villages fail to provide employment to the entire rural folk. Thus the youth flee from their native places with dreams of bright future ahead.

Take a turn; despite being a step towards progress, it has negative impacts that are often overlooked. Firstly, cities are bursting with a large population; migration to cities further puts immense pressure on the limited resources in urban areas. The influx of people increases the demand for housing, food, water, and electricity, which city authorities may not be able to provide effectively. This ultimately leads to a strain on the city's infrastructure, causing the cost of living to go up and creating more challenges for the residents.

Secondly, villages are supposed to be the backbone of our nation but on the verge of losing their worth. The migration of youth from rural areas to cities leads to the loss of valuable skills, knowledge, and labor in the countryside. The out flow is of people who are young and ambitious. They leave behind an aging population and limited skilled labor which prove disastrous for the development of rural areas.

To wind up, while this move may seem like a step towards a bright future, it is difficult to deny that the mass migration of young people to cities has several negative consequences. The cities are thriving under the pressure of new influx and alternatively the rural areas are getting washed off of its significance.

AFFLUENT
WEALTHY

VERITABLE
UNQUESTIONABLE

ELITE
EDUCATED

LUCRATIVE
BENEFICIAL

INSURMOUNTABLE
IMPOSSIBLE

DENOUNCE
CONDEMN

SKEPTICAL
DOUBTFUL

VICISSITUDES
ALTERATIONS

BACKLASH
REACTION

VEHEMENTLY
STRONGLY

GLEAN
GATHER

REPERCUSSION
CONSEQUENCE

ONUS
BURDEN

APPARENTLY
EVIDENTLY

SOPORIFIC
DULL

64

Nowadays, people of all ages from certain parts of the world spend the most time at home rather than going outdoors. Discuss the reasons, is this a negative or positive development?

The societies undergo changes from time to time and it generally happens because of the adjustments in human behavior. Spending most of the time at home instead of going out is a noticed trend of present general public. There are some compelling reasons and I personally would not take it as a healthy change for the society.

The first reason on my tip is the covid pandemic time which has forced most of the working class people to work from home. Since it was compulsory for all to be indoors at that dark phase of life, today people have made it a way of life and finding it more comfortable to stay in and work.

Thinking of next, the maddening crowd, rushy lanes, long waiting hours, unfortunate mishaps on the roads, insecure life, crime rise etc. are some other factors which are avoided by people today quite deliberately by staying in.
Most importantly, modern man does not feel like exhausting himself by rushing out again and again when technology can fulfill his all needs at his home. For example, why he will go to market for daily groceries when order can be delivered at his door step.
Continuing, even sources of entertainment are there at his home and he is not left with the craze of going to clubs, pubs

or movie theaters. As regard meeting friends and folks, they too are always in touch with him through social media and thus he has hardly any obdurate reason to go out.

The trend of spending time indoor is irrefutably a disconcerting change. Because firstly, people today are not experiencing the work place culture and thus becoming self centered and self obsessed somewhere. Secondly, local markets today do not exhibit the hustle bustle as it would experience in the past and also seriously affecting the local trade. Thirdly, inspite of all advantages of technology, dependence on machines for recreation and amusement has given birth to many health issues.

Last not least, indoor culture has put man in the virtual world of monotony with no real peals of laughter.

To end up, modern man has chosen to be indoors for some unavoidable reasons but we cannot deny that this is not a good change. As present society is missing the togetherness of friends, local business has reached the verge of shutting down and virtual world has added to the dullness of life.

The media is increasing interest in famous people who have ordinary backgrounds. Why do you think people are interested in the lives of famous people? Do you think this is a good thing?

Media plays a significant role not only bringing the latest happening around the globe but also bringing featured programs on well renowned people of the society. There are some clear reasons behind people's inclination towards these big shots of the society. For me definitely there is nothing wrong if the life of these great artists is brought to public interest.

First, touching the zenith of success remains a dream of everyone but the struggle and strife of life makes people give up easily. So they remain curious to know how these ordinary people stepped the ladder of success. They feel themselves connected with them to know that even their journey to success was not easy.

Second, Since words of successful people are always heard of very seriously by common man, media people arrange chat shows or celebrities are invited for motivational speeches. People exhibit great interest with the hope that they may get some magic mantra from their talks which may also prove valuable for them. For example, their words, speeches like "I think it is possible for ordinary people to choose to be extra-ordinary." work as motivation agent for

65

them and a common man takes a stride in hunt of his dreams.

Most importantly, every one today desires to have the best lifestyle. If they follow their favourite celebs, they are more like to upgrade themselves in their makeup looks, dressing style, fitness and eating routine etc.

Finally, I perceive that it is good if people show interest in the life of superheroes as to have some role models in life is like to have some source of inspiration and moreover these superman also keep their followers grounded by telling the darker side of their life as they too were the face of the crowd when they started their career.

At this point of day, media highlights the life of well known people of society because common people want to know more and more about them. People show interest in their lives for all above mentioned reasons and I personally appreciate this because people get to know the hard side of celebrities' life, they improve their life style by following them and prominently they take motivation from their tales.

Think, believe, perceive, opine, say, suggest, declare, admit, accept etc are some verbs you use to express your ideas.

 In many countries, people now wear western–style dress such as suits and jeans rather than traditional clothing. Why is this? Is this a positive or negative development?

Countries around the globe have their own traditions and culture in terms of the attires they wear. However the faddy dress fair prevalent today is dominated by western culture which is making people steer away from their customary clothing. There are some precise reasons behind the new trend and I personally believe that this new shift is a good change.

The most vivid reason behind the trend is that modern people are more or less after new fashions and easy availability of western wears motivates them to make it their style. Besides this, many times while being in those countries, they prefer their dressing sense in order to become the part of their culture and feel at home.

In addition, comfy level is another reason for which people prefer these costumes. Though traditional dresses have their own significance but they are not easy wears for jobs and daily chores. For example, it is quite obvious, instead of wearing long sarees or sherwani, a young couple would prefer top and jean as their office wear or on their trip to some wonderland.

Then I perceive that this is positive change. Firstly, the most acceptable truth is that good wear not only enhances the personality of a person but also adds to his great confidence. Modern youth is more poised and has no hesitation in interacting with the people of any community. Secondly, because of easy wears present worker is very much at ease and has not to face the ache of edgy wear. Importantly, it can also be looked upon as a positive change, when the dressing style becomes standard and uniform in nature; it brings a sense of equality among people.

To be very precise, there are some clear reasons why people are adopting western culture in their dressing sense. I definitely take it as a decent break because this easy wear is adding to the confidence of the youth besides bringing uniformity in the societies globally.

67

In most parts of the world, people are living longer. What are the possible causes of this situation? Is this a negative or positive development?

As medical science reveals, life expectancy has roughly tripled over the course of human history. There are some reasons behind it and candidly speaking it is not a very welcoming idea for some grave issues related with it.

To begin with, the greatest reason of long life is advanced medical system which has conquered many diseases today. An infant death rate has been controlled and the most vital part of body, heart can be transplanted. Gone is the time when people would lose life at the outbreak of some epidemic as today vaccination programs are being run successfully which not only save people from untimely deaths but also ensures long healthy life.

In addition, modern man having being aware of his fitness would avoid everything that could be detrimental to his health. Taking nutritious diet, avoid drinking and smoking, having routine for work out, doing stress relieving exercises and staying happy are some of the magic mantras that are helping him enjoy long life.

One another conducive factor is the environment, he is living in. For example, there are some wonderful part on earth which are still not poisoned by the pollution and thus people living there are believed to go for long innings of life.

Alternatively, longevity has serious consequences like it leads to overpopulation. This results in a high demand for food, water, shelter, and other vital resources. The earth's resources are already scarce and an increase in the population leads to the depletion of natural resources.

Secondly, longevity leads to the increased burden on the healthcare system. Weak immune systems make the elderly more susceptible to health complications which makes them dependent on health system.

Thirdly, as people live longer lives, there will be fewer young people to support the elderly. This puts a strain on the economy as the government needs to allocate resources to provide pensions and other benefits to the aging population.

In conclusion, the average life expectancy has increased dramatically over the years, with the advancements in medical technology, people's awareness towards fitness etc. but strangely it is not looked upon as good change as longevity results in over population which in turn bring a toll of other problems too.

68

Many people spend money and not save it. What are the reasons? Is it a positive or negative development?

It has commonly been observed that supervision of an individual's regular income is a great challenge and sometimes saving is neglected or given low priority. Some people overlook the importance of having a culture of saving and generally consume whatever they get from their regular income. This essay aims to examine the causes of the present human behavior and will scan if it is a positive or a negative change.

Focusing on the first reason, Individuals' spending are increasing irresistibly as it is a time of consumerism where he is tempted to buy everything he sees in the market feeling the desperate need of it.

In addition, his social status is another driving force behind it. Being highly class conscious, he would spend blindly buying things of exorbitant price so that he could prove himself successful in the society.

Furthermore, today he wants to enjoy his life to the fullest and goes around on trips and travels to explore the visiting places of the world which unquestionably hardly allows him saving his income.

Answering the next part of the question, lavish spending should not be taken as the negative side of the story. There are also valid reasons for the same. Like their habit of buying keeps the money in rotation and makes the society economically strong.

Then after, a status conscious person contributes significantly in the wealth of nation in terms of paying taxes. With his every purchase good sum gets added to the government's treasury.

Last not least, tours to different places not only make people see the world but also bring all the benefits of tourism to the state.

To sum up, saving is not a culture with many people today for the reasons discussed above and keeping in mind all facts, the 'earn and spend' habit of people can be taken as a positive development as it keeps money in circulation, makes people pay tax on their purchase and brings all advantages of sightseeing.

Make appropriate use of Adverbs as it enhances the meaning and volume of sentences. like :
beautifully, deliberately, rapidly, madly, unexpectedly, dramatically etc

Pick the ADVERBS used in the essay.

69

Some car manufacturing companies have stated that there is a possibility that we will see flying cars in the future. Why is this going to happen? Will it be a positive or negative development?

It is fairly assumed that flying cars are the next big things which are more likely to dominate the future mode of transportation. Automobile industries have declared the likelihood of having winged vehicles in the next few years. The change is expected for some reasons and I believe it will be a positive change.

To begin with, there are some serious reasons behind the need of air-cars. Currently, traffic congestion is the norm in many cities during rush hours, leading to long travel times and frustration for commuters. People want to save time and reach their destination much faster. They wait for wonder cars provided that they enhance the efficiency of their daily lives.

Secondly, the need of such vehicles are highly felt where there are many challenging or inaccessible terrain where either it takes a lot of time and uncomfortable tour to reach or the area remains neglected. For example, flying cars are required for emergency responders who need to get to a location quickly but cannot due to geographical barriers such as mountains or lakes.

Answering next, innovation in the transportation industry is always welcomed and flying cars will be a positive change as they will change the way we travel. Traffic congestion is a major issue in many cities and this innovation will provide a solution to this problem by reducing traffic on the road. With the help of advanced technology, these cars will make the commuters reach the destination faster than traditional road transport. This will save time and also reduce the stress during daily commute. There use will be realized at emergency or during weather disasters, the flying vehicles will be a big help to rescue the victims.

To conclude, future holds great inventions in the field of transportation and aero-cars are needed to ease the daily rush of vehicles on the road and to reach inaccessible lands around the cities. The change should be taken as positive as it will be a solution to traffic congestion, travelers will reach their destination faster and importantly cars will be unexpectedly an aid in emergency rescue operations.

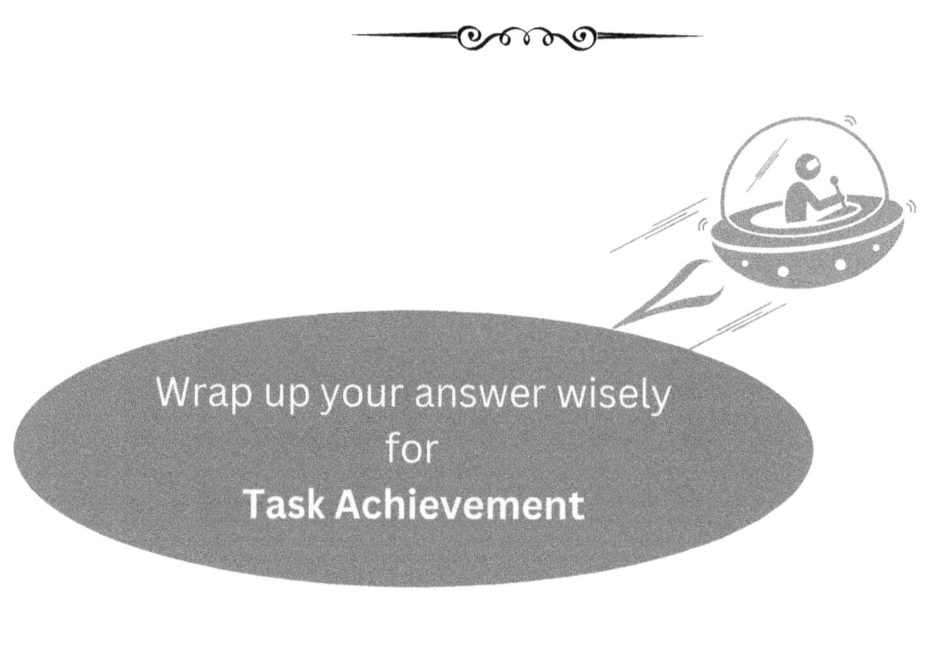

70

Weddings are getting bigger and more expensive. What is the reason for this ? Is this a positive or negative development ?

Marriage is an important event in everyone's life. It is observed that people love to spend lavishly on these special occasions of life. I believe this is happening primarily to a mindset that parents earn mainly to spend on their kids' wedding and to make the event memorable. This growth is certainly not a healthy shift for the society.

To embark on, there is no denying the fact that wedding functions have expanded over the days. The marriage functions today is not a game of a day and a few hours, as in the past when the couples would recite some mantras or exchange their rings and were declared husband and wife. Youth at present time want to make these events unforgettable cherishing memories of life. Moreover the functions start many days before and last longs for a couple of weeks together.

In addition, the show consumes an exorbitant sum of money. Magnificent wedding venues with variety of delicacies and decoration are arranged to give a grand welcome to the marriage procession may be with inclination to display their affluent status.

Nevertheless, the recent upswing in the investment in weddings gives rise to a financial burden for some families. Heavy loans are taken by people to emulate the ostentations. The demands of children have also taken wings not really realizing the financial capabilities of their parents. The superfluous shows dry all the lifelong saving of parents not realizing that the amount could be saved and used for the new life of the couple. Thus scanning the repercussions the growth cannot be awarded as healthy trend.

To conclude, the trend of marriages is gaining in size and expenditure is due to parents' conventional approach and their desire to solemnize all rituals in grand celebrations. There is no justification for such mega shows and thus I can stop writing by stating that it is an unhealthy growth for the society.

Preface

It is time to practice questions now. before you try yourself, there are a few more mixed type of questions. Have a final look at it and then practice all different type of questions by yourself.

You need to understand every question that you pick to practice carefully and have to plan your ideas to answer what has been asked. Always remember that no answer is wrong as it is up to you how do you look at some situation. The only important notable point is how convincingly with grammatical accuracy and with lexical range you can develop your essay.

EASY TIPS
FOR
COMPLEX SENTENCES

Make reasonably long sentences

Children read books in order to improve their general knowledge.

Make Use of Time Linkers

While making plans, it is essential to balance time for everything.

Make use of formal words

Many people **do not** understand the importance of language skills.

Write grammatically correct sentences

When it comes to reducing gas emissions, some measures should be taken.

Write relevant example

The most apt example is of hiking proportion of online study platforms. etc.

AMRITASHAAN

People in the past lived a long and healthy life. Give some reasons why they lived longer. What should the society do to use the ability of elderly people in a positive way?

One of the fascinating findings among historians is that people seemed to have lived longer and healthier in the past. The essay will examine some of the reasons why people had prolonged life in the past and how their services can be availed in a positive way.

First and foremost, people in the past used to lead a very active life physically as most of the household chores were performed manually which helped them stay fit and fine. To make it clear, people instead of using buses, they would prefer to reach their place of work by walk.

In addition, people in the past had nutritious diet where there was no adulteration, pure milk, organic vegetables, fresh air, clean water and pollution free environment would add to their immunity giving them strength to fight with the diseases. Even in face of some health issue, the home remedies or extract of herbal plants were used to cure the disease or heal the wound.

Importantly, the secrete of long and healthy life lies in stress free life full of happiness and that was the natural way of living for the people in the past.

As regard the positive use of their services, knowledge and experience they accumulate over the years, can be used to guide the contemporary society to run the complex social structure. They can be of great use is in the realm of education and mentoring and guiding the youth for their career and sharing with them the expertise they have earned.

Admittedly, an older family member can be a mentor, encouraging and inspiring a younger child to chase their dreams. Their stories of adversity help children to realize that life can be navigated through determination and hard work.

To wrap up, people in the past used to enjoy longer life span for their healthy lifestyle. Notably, even in this stage of life their knowledge can benefit the society and new generation.

Do not use memorised language, phrases and examples.

Some people believe that people who read books can develop more imagination and language skills than those who prefer to watch TV. To what extent do you agree or disagree?

People remain interested in honing their creative skills and language skills through different sources. It is generally observed that these skills can better be enhanced by reading books than by watching shows on television. I do no find the judgment to be very fair as both the sources have their significant role in making people attain accomplishment in the skills.

Talking about the role of books, they are believed to be the greatest source of knowledge and information where the words carry the power to create pictorial world in a reader's mind. The stories transport the readers into the world of imagination and the see the things happening on the screen of their mind. Reading works as a catalyst which ignites the power of fantasizing. For example, a child while reading some chapter of history visualizes the event and thus goes imaginative.

Moreover, reading books is always recommended in order to improve the language skills. The more one reads, the more he comprehends the radicals of the language. The words, phrases, collocations used in articles add to the word power of the readers.

Focusing on the efficacy of watching TV which is unfairly regarded only as an idiot box of entertainment. I tend to believe that when viewers watch different programs; their minds get engaged and start weaving stories of possible happenings. Instead of reading travelogues many people watch channels telecasting panoramic views of world famous landscapes which seize their imagination. The quiz shows serve as an efficient learning tool to enhance analytical competence of mind.

Secondly, the role of TV in boosting linguistic aptitude is exceptionally unparallel too. Exhibition of programs in different languages make people understand different dialects, contributing significantly to linguistic proficiency.

To wrap up, while the benefits of reading are undeniable, they cannot overshadow the role of television in enhancing a person's dexterity at mental agility and language skills.

SOME GOOD WORDS

GENERALLY

LARGELY

HABITUALLY

UNIVERSALLY

OCCASIONALLY

CONSISTENTLY

CLEARLY

PRECISELY

PERFECTLY

RAPIDLY

ULTIMATELY

SCRUPULOUSLY

METICULOUSLY

KNOWINGLY

CATEGORICALLY

In cities and towns all over the world the high volume of traffic is a problem. What are the causes of this and what actions can be taken to solve this problem?

High volume of traffic leading to traffic congestion is an ever increasing problem faced by different cities around the globe. The essay aims to examine the serious causes of the same and would also look for possible cures for the same.

At the outset, with the advent of new technology, more and more luxurious vehicles have been launched in the market at pocket friendly price which has multiplied the number of cars and bikes drastically.
Gone are the day when whole family would commute together on cycle or by a car. Today every member of a family has his own conveyance and would use it as it is affordable for the average consumer.

The second reason is that the introduction of new infrastructure and construction work at rapid speed at different junctions of the cities to meet the hiking need of the daily travelers. If some road is under repair or construction, the moving traffic is expected to face the problem of traffic jam.
One another reason may that society, in general, has become more mobile which is another reason of overcrowding the city lanes.

73

Realizing the gravity of the problem, it is imperative to work on its solutions. One possibility can be to improve the reliability of public transport to encourage people to take the bus or the train rather than get in the car.

It would also be possible to discourage people from driving to work by introducing special tariffs for using the roads, especially during peak periods. A successful pattern of this is the Heavy Parking Charge scheme in Singapore, which has certainly discouraged the use of private bikes.

In conclusion, there are many factors leading to rising levels of traffic in city areas. If above discussed proposals are reviewed, the growing problem of traffic congestion may be trapped for the good of all commuters.

Most of the people do not care enough about environmental issues. To what extent do you agree or disagree with the statement?

Take care of the land, the land will take care of you. Destroy the land and the land will destroy you. This is an acceptable fact and there is a belief that ecological issues are not very much bothered by the people. I do not find it right to put this blame on every person as there are many who are very much concerned about nature and put their sincere effort to protect it.

Focusing on people's point of view, surely, the world is made of all types of people and those who do realize the importance of nature, hardly get time to stand and stare the beauty of breath-taking flora and fauna all around.

In addition, instead of giving any solution, they would contribute in hiking the pollution by making excessive use of their mobiles, air conditioners, bikes and cars, avoiding the public transportation.

Furthermore, disastrous deforestation is a live example how ignorant the people are towards nature.

Last not least, all splendid place of nature are being used as tourists' spots and the pollution, contamination, filthiness and infections, they add to the area always remain a matter of deep concern for the environmentalists.

74

Alternatively, I perceive, since most of the inhabitants of the society are educated, they take every possible measure to keep nature intact. Starting with, the tree plantation, arrangement of kitchen gardens, terrace gardens, organic farming, green Deepawali, where they avoid bursting of crackers are a few vivid steps taken by them to save environment.

Secondly, the large scale campaign where common people are made aware of the significance of every drop of water, use of public transport, boycott of non-biodegradable substances, use of reusable products are some practices followed by many responsible stratum of the society. Apparently, the use of paper has been reduced and people have grown very mindful what and how they have to throw their trash. List is still long but I believe that these reasons are sufficient to prove that our globe is still safe in many hands.

To sum up, though, a few may not realize how imperative it is today to take care of our surroundings, I strongly opine that our the earth is alive and will revive to its original beauty because there are many minds who are working in different ways so that our Mother Nature remain uninjured.

 Many people prefer to spend all the money they earn and not save anything. What are the reasons for this? Is this a positive or negative development? Give reasons for your answer and include any relevant examples from your own knowledge or experience.

Though a few people in society may be economically conservative but it is observed generally that luxury spending of all earning is more common. There are some transparent reasons behind this prodigality and I would take this trend of immoderate expenses as an unhealthy budge.

First and foremost, modern man is a part of consumer ridden society where he is tempted everyday with new products launched in the market. Instead of being satisfied with the goods he already has with him, he would put in his cart the new one for his gratification. How he can be expected to be prudent in spending when there are options for new food, new dresses, new destinations all the time; definitely there is no escape.

Speculating next, living in the present, may be the way of life for many. When future is uncertain, what is the use of saving the earnings. They are of the mindset that time going on is the supreme reality and it should be lived in the dreamt and desired way. For example, increasing trend of visits to tourists' places vividly makes it clear that modern man loves spending lavishly instead of putting the green in the lockers.

75

Then indeed this trend is surely not a positive shift. Like to begin with, since life is very uncertain and insecure, there may be the need of good money any time and thus non – saving personal policy may create helpless situation putting someone in dire need of funds. The people can face emergency situations of life like accidents, diseases etc. provided that they have saved their pay packets. Making it more clear, having handsome savings in bank, my uncle recently could undergo heart transplant surgery otherwise doctors had declared it a gone case.

Summarizing, the habit of overspending is clearly widespread and consumerism is the main mind behind it besides their belief in living in the present. Importantly, I take this as a negative approach because in time of need, the compulsive shopper find their coffer empty and themselves in paralyzed situations.

Personal example should be included if is asked in the question

76 **Today many people choose to be self employed, rather than to work for a company or an organization. Why might this be the case? What could be the disadvantages of being self employed?**

Being self employed is not a career choice, it is a lifestyle choice. Today there is a great number of people who instead of getting hired by some company prefer to be their own boss. There can be some sensible reasons behind their choice but the drawbacks related with, need to be discussed too.

One of the primary reasons of being self-employed is that the people do not want to be a slave to anyone. Sitting at the steering wheel of ship and making people work under them, is something that fascinates them. Instead of giving their time and energy to others, they prefer invest it in their own work. The concept offers the people the freedom to chart their plans by themselves, set their own rules and regulations, choose their clients and projects and be the king of their empire.

For example, self-employment provides the freedom to do any work, he can arrange time for socializing, for his family and importantly for himself and his hobbies. A self-employed person is always full of life and on the go, with no fear of retirement.

Another reason for choosing self-employment is the potential for financial gain. They believe that with their creative ideas, skills, dedication, devotion and passion, they can take their business to the zenith of success.

Alternatively, self-employment is not all a bed of roses as it seems to be. Its disadvantages are shocking and worth considering. First, self-employed people have to wear great work stress and they are never at peace as mind remains occupied with professional responsibilities.

Secondly, self-employed individuals miss out on employer benefits such as health insurance plans, paid time off and retirement benefits. Not to talk about the accountability of making business stand in market and facing the daily challenges and above all facing the situation when competitors outnumber the clients.

To wrap up, inspite of having the option of joining any company as an employee, many decide to opt for self-employment. The alluring reasons have been mentioned above but fact cannot be ignored that challenges it brings with it can put the person under great mental stress.

Always write your answer in your original natal language.

77 **Leaders and directors in an organisation are normally older people. Some people think having a younger leader would be better. Do you agree or disagree?**

The present working scenario generally has senior members at the head positions in different companies and organizations. The notion that supplanting them with their young counterpart would lead to better result, is an approach by a section of society. However I do not take it as a good idea and will try to clear my point of view.

To begin with, I firmly believe that age significantly matters when it comes to the posts of accountability and dignity. The pros and cons of different state of affairs that a senior knows, is something that may put a neophyte in troublesome position, if he is made to sit at the chair of a director or a leader.

In addition, having being in job for a long, the senior folk get excessive knowledge of work and company and thus they provide the customers with consistency and personal attention which is conducive in retaining the clientage intact. For example business magazines often speak about how the customers appreciate seeing long-time workers and feel like visiting same commercial place to enjoy special treatment from the familiar faces.

Alternative, if I think of the role of young leaders in association, they are more likely to be driven by emotions and they lack wisdom, maturity and patience which is not a good attribute for any leader or a head officer in any company. Inspite of having the latest knowledge, they cannot be as proficient at work as an elderly folk because skills develop with time only.

One another reason is that instead of working with uniformity, the youth jump into decisions in order to bring quick results. They want to change the world overnight with their youthful energy often resulting in taking things back gear.

To concise, authoritative positions in different organizations should be under the administration of senior staff because their knowledge at work, consistency and experience are of no match whereas I would not agree with the notion that young leaders could better hold position because in young age they lack the virtues which are needed to be at top position.

Learn to write effective example; Avoid vague survey reports.

SOME GOOD WORDS

PREDATOR
KILLER

SUSTENANCE
LIVELIHOOD

TERMINATION
CLOSE

ESTEEMED
RENOWNED

FORTITUDE
FEARLESSNESS

PERPETUAL
EVERLASTING

ANTIPATHY
DISGUST

LASSITUDE
LAZINESS

EMPATHY
COMPASSION

INCOMPETENCE
INCAPABLE

ARBITRATIONJ
UDGMENT

JURISDICTION
ADMINISTRATION

BASH
CELEBRATION

EPITOME
ROLE MODEL

INFLATION
PRICE
INCREASE

78

Nowadays, a growing number of people with health problems are trying alternative medicines and treatments instead of visiting their usual doctor. Why this is the case? Do you think this is a positive or a negative development?

The ancient or alternative treatments are being in practice for a long time and the trend has been seen in a sturdy hike as regular medical practitioners are being avoided over some alternative cure. I am going to view the reasons behind the growth and my perception makes me believe that this is a positive development since alternative Ayurvedic medicines are showing exceptional results in curing people.

First, since nature is believed to have many herbs, plants and fruits etc. with great healing power which might goad someone to choose alternative medicine than visiting a doctor. It is quite genuine desire as natural treatments are not only safer and gentler but also long lasting than pharmaceutical drugs.

Secondly, while it is true that many pharmaceutical therapies are highly expensive and not within the reach of a common man. They look for some other alternatives and thus Ayurvedic treatments and home remedies emerge as the substitute. Importantly, these treatments are also proving highly successful in curing thousands of people even of their chronic diseases.

One most tangible paradigm is the herbal immunity drink which helped many people elevate their resistance power during the dark phase of corona pandemic when no pharmaceutical drug was helping.

Alternatively, dependence of alternative treatments is not a negative change for the society. Many people use Ayurvedic and naturopathic medicines on a regular basis to maintain a healthy lifestyle and find the cost of them pocket friendly.
Secondly, many people who regularly consume normal medicines observe its negative impacts in the long run.

On the contrary, these natural treatments work effectively without any harmful outcome. According to the latest medical research, it is found that people on regular Allopathic medication develop the fear of kidney failure.

To conclude, these alternative methods have proven successful in curing people and increasing number of people are trying out alternative medication rather than consulting the usual doctors. Considering the advantages it has delivered to the users in more ways than one, I believe that this is a robust turn for the society.

79

Some people think that the government is wasting money on the arts and this money could be better spent elsewhere. To what extent do you agree or disagree?

Allocation of funds to the different sectors of life is premeditated by the authorities very prudently. However a section of society holds a view that government's investment for art is simply a misuse of funds and it would be better if the allocated money could be utilized in some other better way. I do not agree with the notion and I have persuasive perspectives to prove my point of view.

To begin with, art has always been an important part of human society since the beginning of time. Like any other sector of society, it is essential as it keeps us connected with our past. It is a visual form of communication and preserve history in static form. For example, an artist paints a picture or sculpts a statue which depicts the life of a famous historical figure. These pieces of art give us a glimpse of the lifestyle and history of our past. These precious static lessons can be in any form of art like painting, statue, building, monument, a dance or in a written form. If the sector is neglected by authorities, the past will not remain alive.

In addition, art in its different forms makes the cities and the towns beautiful. The artists not only get a chance to exhibit their talent but many blooming artists get job opportunities of making cities and towns beautiful with their arty skills. The Rock Garden in Chandigarh is the most tangible paradigm of creativity which has today become the most happening place of city.

Last not least, artistically beautiful countries around the world invite tourism as they have wonder of specimens of art to amaze the tourists. Art not only reflects the architectural development of a society but makes some town a place of great tourist interest. For example, the Taj, the Kutub minar or the Lotus Temple the amazing specimens of art are the recognition of our country where tourism is a source of earning revenue for our country.

To be precise, realizing the benefits of promotion of art in a country, I can firmly reiterate that investment of government's fund in art is not the squandering of money. Rather reserved funds for art should only be used for art because there lies the beautiful development of the society.

The World is but a canvas to our imagination.

80

Some people think that zoos are cruel and should be closed down. Others, however, believe that zoos can be useful in protecting wild animals. Discuss both views and give your opinion.

Zoo is a zoological garden where animals are kept for the exhibition of daily visitors. Despite zoos being quite functional, a group of intellectuals opine that captivating animals in such enclosures is an inhumane act and so better shut them down. Whereas other people stand in contradiction that zoos are always beneficial to shelter wild animals. I will discuss both the views and give my opinion in the conclusion.

On the one hand, zoos are considered to be callous, relentless places which limit the freedom of their animal by providing poor quality environments and facilities. Since it is not their natural habitat, animals fail to have their daily activities which they could do in their territory otherwise. This makes the animals lose their natural instinct and either they grow feeble or they go aggressive and violent which defeats the point of keeping them in the zoo.

Additionally, the animals are teased quite often by the visitors to the zoos in which most of them are kids. The kids, for fun tease them and bother them consistently. On top of that, sometimes visitors feed them the things which are not healthy for them.

For instance, people provide monkeys with sweets which deteriorates monkey's health as artificial sugar is not suitable for them.

On the flip side, keeping the animals in the artificial zoos has some advantages too like some species which are labeled as endangered can be kept safe in the zoos as there would be no fear of potential predators to them. In zoos, these species can be bred and could be protected from being extinct.

Furthermore, zoos work really hard to save the threatened animals as some species are picked up from the woods in order to keep them safe in their premises and to re-introduce them back into their habitat after some time. This helps to keep biodiversity alive.

To sum up, both the groups have their own opinion but I personally believe that keeping animals in zoos is a good idea because animals remain safe from the hunters, endangered species bred well and biodiversity remains intact with the coming back of healthy animals back to their habitats.

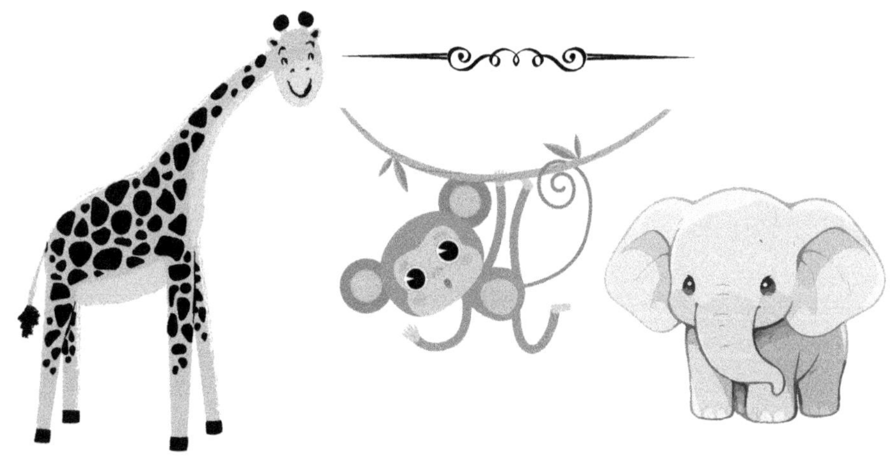

81

Nowadays, more people are choosing to socialize online than face to face. Is this a positive or negative development?

The world has witnessed an exponential growth in the way people communicate with one another today. The traditional mode of communication has shifted from face-to-face to online means where people are inclined to meet their mates virtually. Though traditional way of socializing is on visible decline, yet I find the change to be progressively positive.

Counting the first aspect, socializing online is a time-saving activity as in the present time where everyone is constantly occupied; no one has time to visit their friends and folk personally. The ease of access to various social media platforms allows people to stay connected with their friends and family members while handling their busy schedules. For example, the trend of sending 'Good Morning' message does not take much time but keeps the sweetness of relation fresh.

Secondly, with the growing trend of globalization, socializing online surpasses all physical barriers making it possible to foster relationships with people who are living far from us. A son may be living in Canada or Australia or friend is occupied in Delhi of Mumbai, he is only a click away from his parents today.

Thirdly, learning horizons have been made broader by these communication Medias. Instead of physically moving to a teacher for guidance, one can rather choose online connection and interact with teacher sitting anywhere in the world. The knowledge of new cultures and traditions is something that present generation is experiencing since their social circle is not limited to their local places today. As soon as people register themselves on online platform, they experience that the large world has shrunk in a small global village.

Most importantly, when online incredible things happen like with online interaction many people have successfully launched their business and their online friends helped them multiply their income by sharing the business links with their friends.

In conclusion, socializing online is a way of life today. When it offers numerous advantages like saving time, making easy accessibility to friends and folks for personal or professional reasons, helping people easy trading etc, there is no reason not to accept it as a positive change.

Make Use of Time Linkers

Because of, in As soon as, Similarly, Indeed. Instead etc.

82 **Some people believe that it is important to give gift to friends and family to show that we care about them. Others think that there are some better ways to show that we care. Discuss both the views and give your opinion.**

Giving presents to our near dear ones on their special occasions has been a delightful culture that we have been following since long. A section of society holds a view that giving gift is nice gesture to let someone know how much we are concerned about him while others believe there are other better ways by which emotions can be expressed. Scanning of both the views will help me reach my perception.

To begin with, people who are in favor of giving gifts believe that it is the cutest practice to wrap something in a beautiful glittering paper, write good wishes on it and give it to the special one. Such gestures are appealing way to win hearts and are pleasantly welcomed. The most tangible paradigm is the excitement children exhibit while opening their birthday gift boxes with a feel that there are so many people to shower their love on them.

In addition, many times instead of wrapping a box of chocolate as a gift, something that a person needs is given in order to make one realize that people around him not only know his needs but are also ready to fulfill it. Unforgettably, gift is a token of love.

82

These souvenirs become the part of sweet memory and work to sweeten and strengthen the bonds of relations.

On the flip side, others argues that since everyone is highly occupied in their daily pursuits, sparing time for darlings can be a better option. Sitting with an elderly person, enquiring about his health, telling funny activities of the day would definitely bring happiness for the receiver. For example, a gift of an expensive watch will value nothing for a grandmother who will feel elated simply with the company of her family members.
Last but not the least, special treatment like surprises, picnic trips, arranging day off can also make someone realize that there are people who care concerned about him.

Finally, after scanning both the views I can conclude that the practice of giving gifts is important, provided that a desired thing should be wrapped because this cute practice not only exhibits our love but also helps us fulfill the need of our dear one. The sweetness in relation and loving bonds blissfully remain intact.

The responsibility to prevent global environment damage is on politician rather than individuals. Do you agree or disagree?

The most disconcerting issue to discuss today is comprehensive environmental deterioration which is a result of detrimental human activities. It is assumed that it lies under the jurisdiction of political leaders to take preventive measures to check this destruction in nature and the people have no obligation. I do not consider the idea to be very practical as people can bring pragmatic change with their sensible efforts.

To begin with, I believe that each person has the power and prudence to protect the nature from being getting impaired. Instead of putting things on authorities if every citizen determines not to take any action against environment, the conditions of surroundings can be efficaciously improved. As it is said, "Every drop counts" similarly, every individual needs to be aware of the cause of the problem and be responsible not to practice it.

Additionally, if I talk about the causes of environmental problems, what strikes to mind is global warming which is rising due to the excessive use of fossil fuels that release carbon dioxide in environment. Despite knowing the negative effects of it, people impulsively use these resources

83

at a large scale. For example, to run machines in industries, to rum different appliances at home, for commuting and so on. Lowering down the use of these resources can be the plausible way to address the issue.

Moreover, in this age and time when we need to grow more and more trees to deal with the damage, deforestation is commonly seen to build residential colonies. Nature should not pay for a country's growth. People not only need to understand their roles in protecting the nature but also to help it flourish more. For instance, chipko movement was organized in a village where ladies adamantly stood hugging the trees in order to save them from being cut down in a part of country.

To summarize, sustainability of nature is the dire need of time. So, I believe nature can be preserved by common man's efforts provided that they need to mend their ways and inculcate the habits aforementioned to keep the Mother Nature intact.

Pragmatic change, preventive measures, sensible efforts, residential colonies, dire need etc.
Understand the use of adjectives for impressive vocabulary

84

Some people prefer to spend their lives doing the same things and avoiding change. Others, however, think that change is always a good thing. Discuss both views and give your opinion.

Change means to be progressive in life but it begins at the end of our comfort zone. That is the reason a stratum of society prefers doing same things and they circumvent newness in life. However others fairly stand in favour of freshness in life. I need to scrutinize both the ideas to reach my conclusion.

To begin with, change is inevitable in life but many people avoid it as they are happy to be in easy zone when they know what will happen next. Having being accustomed to their daily lives, people fear that change to this routine could bring uncertainty and may upheaval their life badly. For example, leaving a permanent job and starting one's own business is something that may not be considered a wise change by many.

To add on, the fear of failure makes many stay in the circumstances they have been in. A change can be stressful or challenging. The fear of the unknown and the associated risks stop people from making a shift. Since they already have the taste of it, they keep following the beaten path with a relaxed state of mind that there will be no disaster on the way.

On the contrary, the people who think out of the box love to embrace transformations in life as they see the benefitting aspects of it. If a person enters a unseen zone, he is most like to have new challenges, risks, as no new road of life is smooth to walk on but he not only grows bold enough to accept hurdles of life but learns from his mistakes and failures.

Next, the change lovers reasonably argue that life will be very monotonous, dull and dreary if one has to follow same set to routine for a long time. Change brings a sense of renewal and rejuvenation to our lives. It encourages us to live life fully, with passion and purpose, and to never stop exploring new possibilities.

Finally, I perceive that the views related with the discussion have logic reasons, fear of new uneasy circumstance may retards many bringing newness in life but I would like to accept changes in life and reason are quite clear that it makes people more flexible for new situations and keep adding fresh flavor to life.

85

Some people think that government should decide the subjects for students to study in university other believe that student should be allowed to apply for the subject they prefer. Discuss both views and give your opinion.

Whether the emphasis should be on compulsory subjects or hand-picked courses at the time of university study, is a topic of hot discussion. Though some individual think that government should decide the subjects for students while others propose to leave the students at their choice. In my opinion, students themselves can surely better decide the stream for themselves since they are more concerned and dedicated toward their future.

To begin with, a section of society believes that academic stream of study for individuals should be decided by the ruling authorities. As the most burning issue of unemployment will be solved. For instance, government will provide lessons to the students in that sectors where need of employees is more and this can be achieved by making students take the subjects which authorities put in the list. Consequently positive impact of development would be seen in respiring industrial sectors.

Secondly, if authorities provide subjects, they can balance most of the students from following the rat race where they disappointingly find themselves only in the list of educated unemployed.

Turning to the other view, where the suggestion is for self

selection of subjects of study. Firstly, it is indisputable fact that person provides better results if they are working in the field of their interests. For instance, there are personalities who have achieved a great success in their preferred field even though there was a limited chance of success.

Moreover, the process of self-selection creates the sense of freedom and responsibility which may be a blaming sector with other option. Another big reason is that nowadays students are more aware of pros and cons of different streams because they explore and extract all knowledge and information from different Medias on internet. Thus they are prudent enough to decide what the best is for them.

Generally speaking, both the ways of choosing subjects are important but in my opinion, students should choose their subjects with their own perception because when they choose according to their choice they will study with more dedication and put more efforts to shape their future.

You are free to givee your opinion what you feel is right. Your answer will only be examined on the basis how relevantly it has been explained.

86   **In the future, there will be higher proportion of older people than young people in many countries. Is it positive or negative development?**

While it is essential to respect and care for our elderly population, it is crucial to acknowledge the potential challenges that a higher population of old people may bring. It is genuinely feared that older population will take over the younger ones in many countries in coming years and I am inclined to believe it will be quite precarious situation and thus be unhealthy growth for the society.

To begin with, since diseases, health issues come uninvited with old age, a higher population of old people can seriously burden healthcare systems. The hospitals, clinics will remain over crowded with ailing people and long waiting times, inadequate resources, and overburdened medical staff will have to compromise with their sincere services. For example, researchers instead of making new inventions, finding new cures and remedies will be busy giving life support to the aged people lying on their hospitals beds.

Another perturbing concern is that an aging population can lead to an imbalance in the labor market. As more old people approach retirement age, there may be a shortage of skilled workers in various sectors. This shortage can hinder economic growth and development by restricting the availability of experienced professionals.

Additionally, a higher population of old people can create heavier economic burden on government sector. A great proportion of government's treasury will be consumed allocating monthly pensions, medical insurances charges or other retirement benefits. The graph of tax payees will have such a slump that younger individuals will have to face challenges for their economic well-being.

In conclusion, the increasing population of old people is seen as a negative development in society. The rationale behind this viewpoint is that it places additional strain on healthcare systems, leads to an imbalance in the labor market, and results in harder economic burden where younger generation will have to go extra miles for their financial fitness.

These are the suggested answers which can help you score required high bands.

87 **Nowadays young people are spending most of their leisure time using smart phones and tablets for amusement. Is it a positive or negative development? Give your opinion.**

In the contemporary era, it is indisputable that smartphones and comparable technologies are integral to human society. Presently, the younger generation's leisure time is noticeably dominated by smartphones and tablets. Personally, I perceive this as an adverse trend and i will elaborate on my views in subsequent paragraphs.

To commence with, smart phone is a great distraction and can also become an addiction if not used responsibly. Teenagers nowadays, instead of studying, spend their time religiously with their phones. The constant rings and ongoing notifications do not let a person sit idle even for a second and do not let him focus anywhere else. On the top of that, the blue light emitted by the smart phones can sometimes also disrupt natural sleeping patterns of an individual. This can lead to the person not being able to fall asleep easily or in some cases, not even getting any sleep. Fatigue, irritation and peevish temper, grumpy demeanor become common in these avid phone users.

At the extreme edge, I believe that smart phones, overall, can lead to loneliness. Though, smart phones make connectivity with friend and family easier, it can also lead to isolation as people spend most of their time on phones, the social skill in them depletes overtime. To exemplify, teenagers nowadays hesitate to talk to anyone in an open space. Since they spend most of their leisure time on phones and tablets playing games so there is no way to enhance social intelligence or extroversion. This can also make them feel disconnected from others.

In conclusion, I find the widespread use of smartphones to be predominantly detrimental. It promotes distractions from academic pursuits, fosters self-isolation resulting in feelings of loneliness and gives rise to health issues for users.

Every essay goes with its own vocabulary ; so do not force the learnt words into your writing.

SOME GOOD WORDS

SKEWED
DISTORTED

JURISDICTION
AUTHORITY

CONSEQUENTIAL
IMPORTANT

PRECARIOUS
RISKY

METICULOUS
THOROUGH

AFFINITY
FELLOW FEELING

STAID
SERIOUS

FOSTER
PROMOTE

ANTAGONISTIC
AGGRESSIVE

CONTEMPLATE
THINK

ERODE
FADE

CONGENIALITY
FRIENDLINESS

PIVOTAL
ESSENTIAL

EXECRABLE
DISGUSTING

DIGRESS
GO OFF THE POINT

88

Young people committing crimes should be treated the same as adults by the authorities. To what extend do you agree or disagree?

A serious rise in juvenile delinquency is regretfully prevailing in society on today's date. There is a suggestion that authorities should discipline young criminals in the same way that they do with the grownups. With reservations, I do concur with the statement.

To commence with, castigating them in the same way will set down an example for other potential criminals. If the young offender is punished fairly, the others will be made aware of the severe consequences. This can reduce the crime rate among the young considerably as the budding offender will know that the rule of the land is not going to spare them and they can be granted with harsh punishment for any damage they do to the society.

In addition, there is no concrete reason not to punish them equally if they are found involved in some evil doing, it means, they have devil minds and age is only a mitigating factor which can set down a notion in their minds that no matter what crime they commit, they are not going to be held accountable for it for they are underage. To epitomize, juvenile criminal cases can be seen at an alarming rate where law is compassionate towards young criminals.

Alternatively, I believe that punishing them to the same degree may not always be right. There are some things that can trigger the young ones to commit a crime.

For instance, he could do an inappreciable deed in a spur of emotions like anger or sadness. Instead of having a bad intention, it could simply be a mistake. Furthermore, a severe punishment can also scars the young one's life and the stigma could ruin his all chances of reformation. Placing them in Juvenile prisons for a period of time instead can be the perfect rehabilitation spots for them.

To sum up, although, penalty is important but I judge that reprimanding tool for adolescents should not be same as that of adults as they are in the tender age of their life. Instead rehabilitation plan by keeping them away from common stream of life for time can be a right judgment.

Some times candidates use vocabulary that they think will impress the examiner.
This results in incoherent writing because those words do not sound apt in that particular situation.

89

Many today feel that most urgent problems can only be solved by international cooperation. To what extent do you agree or disagree?

Natural disasters, world wars and many other serious predicaments are the way of life worldwide. It is believed that nations today need to join hands to deal with emergency situations. I too tend to opine that global cooperation has the ability to effectively address emerging critical circumstances.

First, the significance of international cooperation is direly realized during the time of natural disasters like drought, floods, famine or pandemics etc. when individual nations feel helpless and look at the world to take care of them. Similarly, viruses and bacterial attacks takes a toll of lives in short span of time, the medical aid from different nations can only control the situation from growing worse. The most tangible paradigm is the attack of coronavirus in the recent past which had taken the whole world in its grip in no time and it was finally won over when researches were made by scientists of different nations together.

Second, by joining hand together, different nations emerge as a world power and enjoy the authority to frame rules and regulations for world community. Instead of living in peace, today many countries and most importantly neighbouring nations have environment of animosity. The hardly realize that war brings destruction and spread the poison of hatred everywhere. Different nations can force warring nations to resolve their disputes peacefully.

Considering another issue, if any country goes under the attack of terrorism, the situation is more likely to cause the atmosphere of fear and insecurity, violence and death. This makes civilians feel defenseless in their everyday lives. These type of dire situations can be combated, provided that all nations stand together to co-operate and help the victim nation in handcuffing the rebels. Obliging one another level not only ensures curbing intimidation but promotes the environment of safety and security.

To sum up, there is no denying the fact that the individual countries are too weak to fight against serious global issues. Only cooperation at international level is a remedy owing to the fact that during the time of natural calamities a single nation goes dependent, with mutual cooperation issues of warring nations and terrorism can be combated successfully.

Use the question to help you organize your answer.

Some people believe that sport competitions are a source of emotional stress for young people. Therefore, youth should be banned from participating in sport competitions. Do you agree or disagree?

One of the most disconcerting aspects of society is to see the youth struggling with depression and anxiety today. A stratum of society holds sport competitions responsible for inducing mental pressure among the youth and suggests prohibiting the participation of youth in such antagonistic events. My perspective firmly believes that discouraging young people from engaging in sports activities is an unacceptable notion and my supporting rationale will confirm this belief.

To begin with, the idea of restraining the youth from sports with a fear that it would lead to their anxiety is a baseless apprehension. Rather keeping them away from these activities may have negative affect as their life will become more sedentary in the absence of games and sports. Since sports is believed to be a stress buster activity which provides great fun and helps the player forget the problems of life. Having no enthusiastic activities will invite monotony in life leading to more insipid routine where depression will be a dominating factor.

On the flip side, participation in sports competitions in itself is a lesson to fight against the odds of life. A player is well taught that victory and defeat are the part of life which should be accepted happily.

Failures are taken as the pillars of success and sports persons are exhorted not to take the defeat to heart as life does not end with a failure. Competitions prepare them to face the battle of life and accept life as it comes. Making it more relevant, medical thesis also proves that sport persons are immune to any type of emotional breakdown.

The closing note is that restricting playful competitive activities is not a remedial act of the concerned situation rather it actually equips the youth with physical and mental strength which enables them to cope up with such emotional collapse.

A few proverbs

- All work no play makes Jack a dull boy - Anonymous
- Just play. Have fun. Enjoy the game. - Michael Jordan
- It's not how big you are, it's how big you play. - John Wooden
- I've failed over and over and over again in my life and that is why I succeed. - Michael Jordan

91

Many people spend money and they do not save it. What are the reasons? Is it a positive or negative development?

Quite unquestionably, effectively managing personal finances is essential for achieving financial security in life. It is observed that instead of saving money, many people prefer to squander it. I intend to address its root causes as well as explain my ideas on why it is an unhelpful change.

To commence with, I believe there are many reasons because of which people spend money so profusely today. The most possible is the lack of knowledge on how to or why to save money. Since they are not aware of the importance of saving, they imprudently pay off their monthly rolls. In addition, a person's desire to showcase his luxurious lifestyle is also another staid cause behind the concern. Instead of leading a life of simplicity, they would prefer to tag themselves with different brands. To exemplify, in order to flaunt their high standard, young teenagers usually use up their funds on useless things.

What is more, it is absolutely a negative development if they are not being able to save any money as it is more likely to take them to a situation of financial crisis. For instance, accidents and injuries come uninvited and any such misfortune can require lots of funds, not having any cutback amount, will leave the person in a helpless situation. Having reasonable financial saving will grant a person with a greater sense of security in life.

Additionally, excessive consumerism is also a repercussion of this very development. People are stuffing their wardrobes with everything that is new in the market.

At last, I believe that though spending money may be out of ignorance or gratification of social status, the negative outcome of it should not be overlooked. As it makes a person feel helpless during the bad patches of life and undesirable growth of consumerism leaves its dark side on the society.

A few proverbs

- **Wealth consists not in having great possessions but in having few wants.** – Epictetus

- **When money realizes that it is in good hands, it wants to stay and multiply in those hands.** – Idowu Koyenikan

- **Too many people spend money they haven't earned to buy things they don't want, to impress people that they don't like.** – Will Rogers

- **A penny saved is a penny earned.** – Benjamin Franklin

92

Homelessness is increasing in many major cities around the world. What do you think are the main causes of this problem and what measures could be taken to solve it?

It is quite unfortunate that there are many people who do not have any respectable dwellings to live in. The sight of down-and-out masses is universal today which is a matter of deep concern. Some possible reasons and discreet feat to address the mess will be discussed in the next paragraphs.

At the outset, unmanageable migration of people from rural areas to the urban places is the main cause. Since the mega cities have already reached a point of saturation in terms of accommodating people, the inflow of populace from other areas is leading to the problem. The emigrants go homeless either for less availability of houses or for unaffordable heavy rental prices.

To add on, persisting poverty in the society can be another reason. Though there is unexpected development all around but the bitter fact is that there are many people in the society who are still in impoverished circumstances. When arranging a meal for a day is a question for them, having a reasonable shelter on head is not even in their dreams. For example, the sight of people living on footpaths or under temporary houses in the slums is a heart rending scene of metro cities.

Focusing on the remedial steps, the authorities need to retard the flow of villagers to cities by providing good job opportunities to them in their villages only. Industrial growth in remote areas can be a soothing step. Most importantly, construction of low cost economical shelters by government can make a decent living possible for the deprived stratum of the society.

In conclusion, the problem of homelessness is a sorry affair unquestionably but the reasons behind are quite obvious. If industries are setup in far off places, the inflow to people to cities will surely be controlled. Last, simple dwellings with fundamental provisions will improve the sight of cities by depleting the problem of homelessness.

What is a complex sentence?

A complex sentence is made up of two or three simple sentences to expand an idea or a situation. They form an important aspect of the IELTS writing task to showcase the grammatical range.

Pick complex sentences from the answer paragraphs above and make more practice of writing in complex structure.

93

Some people encourage watching sports as a way of learning about teamwork and strategy, while others believe that one can learn these skills only through playing sports. Discuss both views and give your opinion.

Sports aspirants employ a range of methods to achieve proficiency in their endeavors. A group firmly supports watching sports for getting to know about teamwork and important tactics whereas for others participation in sports is the only key. Detailed debate on both the aspects will help me frame my opinion.

Those who realize the significance of watching sport events hold the opinion that the shows make sports aspirants learn how the players work in complete harmony and follow each other's instructions or gestures even. For example, in football match, it is amazing to see how the players pass the ball to their team members only and opponent team have to strive to reach the ball. Although all these tricks are also taught to them but watching them happening come as a real lesson to them. Besides this, the importance of obedience, discipline and cooperation etc. are some others traits that the players showcase make a learner understands the significance of team work.

The opponents too have their arguments to support the importance of playing a game practically. Through active participation, individuals experience the challenges and complexities of a game as a team and make their strategies to win. Inspite of having all theoretical knowledge, until unless a player experiences, he can neither score a goal and nor he could realize the strength of his rival. For instance, stepping into pool will only make a swimmer know the depth of the pool. Thus undoubtedly, all great virtues and strategies can be better understood if the players are engaged more and more in sports' activities.

After looking at both the arguments, I personally believe though watching sports events provide great lessons that players need to know but we should not forget that practice makes a man perfect. Real limits and possibilities are realized by the players only at play. Since at that time they come in face with situations where they have to take instant decisions and apply the best strategies.

94

New technologies have changed the way children spend their leisure time. Do the advantages of this development outweigh the disadvantages?

The influence of technology is evidently observable in the way children pass their free time today. While this has several benefits, I believe that the drawbacks need to be studied before drawing any conclusion.

Acceptably, the great cognitive development among modern children is perceptibly the result of computer games and other applications that they use most of the time as their holiday activity. Having being techno – savvy, they not only use the applications to interact with their mates but give their free time to understand the use of various new applications which as a result helps them to grow analytically and logically wise.

Additionally, advancement in multi-media has generated the interest of the youth in creative activities as it can be clearly observed from the short reels and videos, photos, and posters etc. they create and upload on the social accounts. Inspite of waiting for some opportunity, they exhibit their talent by making videos in the spare time and enjoy the fun and many times go famous too. The most substantial paradigm is of millions of Instagram reels reels created by youngsters as their fun activity.

Looking at other side, a rose cannot be without a Thorne. Similarly, addiction of social media and distraction from other important activities of life is one of the most concerning aspect of the issue. It further gives rise to many problems like, children today are growing self-centered as they hardly need any friends which is making them lose their social skills. Not to ask of the ill effects of these leisure activities on health. Poor eye sight, bad body postures and obesity are a few of health hazards commonly seen among the addicted kids. One more point to raise is the constraining family time. Gone are the days when family members would sit together at their leisure time enjoying different fun activities. Today the kids are totally in grip of technology for their amusement and somewhere the cordial family ties are losing their sweetness too.

To conclude, though the above discussed concept surely aware the dark side of technology for leisure use but I am of the opinion that positive aspect overshadows as it makes children more sound technically and judiciously. The creative side that comes to light is also the result of their free time involvement in different sources of technology.

95

Some people think that it is necessary to travel abroad to learn about other countries, but others think that it is not necessary to travel abroad because all the information can be seen on TV and the internet. Discuss both views and give your own opinion.

Man has always exhibited the desire and curiosity to explore the places around the globe. A section of society holds an opinion that going around the world tour is necessary to get information about the places. Whilst others negate the importance of travelling, when all information is available on television and internet today. Scanning of both the views will help me reach my judgment.

A school of thought opines that foreign travel is imperative to comprehend about other countries since real life situations and experiences create a stronger imprint in a person's mind than any virtual knowledge about the same. This may be true due the fact that nothing can be more convincing than real life experiences. For example, the beauty of the Taj can only be realized by one who has visited the place as for others it is a monument made of marble. Importantly, if one lands in some particular place, he is more likely to have the real touch, feel, taste of the place.

In addition, it an invaluable way of improving skills, knowledge, and confidence. Going to a different country is a perfect way to find inspiration as it is a great way to learn new things and immerse in a new culture, tradition, fair, festivals and cosines.

The second school of thought is that television is a great source of knowledge and information. A great deal of time and money is invested by the researches in accumulating all important facts about the places and are complied in a documentary. The detailed virtual documentaries are not only a source of entertainment but also provide us with thorough knowledge about the places. For example, the facts and information of world famous forests, deserts, palaces, forts or museums are well documented in different web series. Instead of going to precarious expeditions, it is better to get meticulous knowledge through television or internet.

Finally, although it is not compulsory to travel to a foreign land to learn about it but what I feel is that one can gain a better view about a country only by journeying to that place as real life experience has no comparison with virtual trips. If one wants to have the real touch, feel, taste of the place, he needs to walk through the streets, taste the food and suck in the air of the place.

A few proverbs

"A day of traveling will bring a basketful of learning."
"It is better to see one time than to hear one
hundred times."
"Wisdom can be found traveling."

96 **The tendency of news reports in the media to focus more on problems and emergencies than on positive developments is harmful to the individuals and the society as a whole. To what extent do you agree or disagree? Give reasons for your answer and include any relevant examples from your own knowledge and experiences.**

We live in a world where media plays a significant role in shaping our understanding of the world around us. However, there is growing concern about the harmful effects of media's relentless focus on problems and emergencies. This article will delve into the various ways in which sensationalized news can distort our perception of reality, breed fear and anxiety but at the same time how the exposure of darker side of society is also needed, will be discussed too.

To start with, when the media focuses primarily on problems and emergencies, it creates a skewed perspective where the world appears to be a dangerous and chaotic place, filled with nothing but negativity. This constant exposure to fear-based news can have a profound psychological impact on individuals and can lead to anxiety, fear, and a loss of trust in our society. For example, when youth hears that there is scarcity of jobs and recession will grow worse, fuels the mind of the youth with anxieties and erodes their sense of safety and security.

Looking at the trend from different angle, it comes to light that one crucial aspect of media's function is to focus on problems and emergencies and to bring them to public consciousness by which common masses get alert and take precautionary measures to defend themselves. For instance, the objective of news regarding online bank robberies is not to frighten the people but to caution them regarding their online transactions. Thus media uncovers hidden issues and injustices that may otherwise go unnoticed. Amplifying the voices of those who are often overlooked or marginalized also lies under the jurisdiction of media. Negative news are brought to the forefront of public attention to give a voice to the unheard, raise awareness and spur conversations that can lead to meaningful change.

To close the case, it can be stated that though sensitized news create anxiety and fear in the mind of people but I personally believe that revelation of dark side of society makes public conscious and they take defensive measure, government gets aware and victims get the justice. Media becomes the voice of unheard and consequential changes take place in the society.

Remember

- Your handwriting should be beautiful legible
- Must take care of spelling, write correctly
- High bands require flawless grammatical sentences

SOME GOOD WORDS

VICISSITUDE
CHANGE

PERMEATE
SPREAD
THROUGHOUT

RUDIMENTARY
FUNDAMENTAL

REPLENISH
RENEW

TENTATIVE
UNDECIDED

GESTICULATE
GESTURE

VACUITY
EMPTINESS

BUZZWORDSA
BRACADABRA

AMBIGUOUS
DOUBTFUL

INEXPLICABLE
INCOMPREHEN
SIBLE

REDACT
EDIT

PRECISION
PERFECTION

ANTAGONISTIC
UNFRIENDLY

CIRCUMSPECT
CAREFUL

DESPONDENCY
DEPRESSION

97

Today, many people do not know their neighbors. Why is this? What can be done to improve contact between neighbours?

Our neighbours refer to the families living in close proximity to us, specifically next door to our houses. It is a sorry affair of present society that there are many people who hardly know who dwell in the houses next to them. I firmly believe that it is a result of fast pace life man is in grip of and high-tech society we are living in. By arranging some community programs and with some more measures the social affinity can be ameliorated and same will be elaborated in ensuing paragraphs.

The main reason why there is less interaction with the neighbours is that everyone is highly occupied in the fast running society. Having being aspirant about high goals, no one has time to peep what is happening next door. Seriously, working people leave their houses early in the morning and return late at night are not left with any time for socializing.

Then technology can also be blamed for this wishy - washy scenario of society. Gone are the days when people would sit together with their neighbours in the evening over a cup of tea to relax their minds. Today they have many technical appliances live T.V, mobile etc. to pass their leisure hours. For example, instead of arranging a cricket match in the street, the people will love to watch it on TV and thus they know little about people living pretty near.

This contemporary problem can be dealt with if people themselves realize the importance of their neighbours and spare time to spend with them. By inviting them to their family functions and festivals can surely generate the environment to cordial rapport. One another way could be the arrangement of some community programs where it would be mandatory for locality members to be present and participate. Such meeting can foster the feeling of goodwill and congeniality among all.

To sum up, a little acquaintance with neighbours today is the way of life. No doubt how genuine the reasons may be, i am personally of the view point that amiable efforts should be made to improve the relations. Social get together and celebrations of fair and festival can create opportunity to know good about the people in our vicinity.

98

There is an increasing trend around the world to have a small family rather than a large family. What are some of the advantages and disadvantages of having small family rather than a large family?

A small family refers to a household structure consisting of a limited number of members, typically parents and one or two children. The concept of a small family has gained unique attention in the contemporary society and gone are the days when there would be many members in a family. This article explores the various benefits as well as drawbacks of opting for a small family size.

To begin with the potential merits, a small family reduces the financial burden as with fewer children, parents allocate their financial resources more effectively to the family needs. This means they provide better quality education, healthcare, and overall standard of living for their children. Having a small family allows parents to invest in their own growth, and have a safety net for unexpected expenses. For example, parents with single child not only bring up the child in affluently but also enjoy their respectable saving after retirement.

In addition, in small families parents focus well on nurturing their child's emotional well-being, education and personal growth and this close-knit relationship promotes trust, support and a deeper connection between parents and children. Quality time they spend together may not be possible in families with many members.

Alternatively, the complexities of having a small family needs equal attention. First, it is believed that joys go double and sorrows go less when they are shared with family members. In times of need, having aunts, uncles, grandparents, and cousins to rely on can make a difference. The importance of relations is fading somewhere in the context of small family units.

Second, the child in a small family has to play multiple roles and have to carry a heavier load of responsibilities. Similar lies the case with parents who find themselves juggling multiple roles, leading to stress and overwhelm.
Last not least, it can be quite lonely when one does not have many siblings to hang out. With fewer people around, the options for social interaction within the family are limited which lead to a sense of isolation and a lack of variety in social dynamics.

To recapitulate, the drift of small families goes with both pros and cons. If stable financial structure, better nurturing of kids and strong family bonds are the plus side of the concept, lack of family support, load of liabilities and serious chances of loneliness among kids can be the minus aspects of it.

99

Many people believe that healthy eating and the importance of healthy food should be taught in schools. Others say that parents should teach their kids about healthy food and diet. Discuss both views and give your opinion.

A good diet serves as the essential element for all healing and promoting a healthy lifestyle. Since children in the present time are more to fast food and are not very active in their daily routine, the concerned stratum of society gets divided in two opinions regarding who should teach young generation about eating habits. My essay will probe in to both the concern to reach some final decision.

It is believed to be essential for schools to prioritize teaching about healthy eating because in the time when there are so many food choices, children are not astute enough to understand what is healthy eating. If these lessons are incorporated in school curriculum, they are more likely to understand that energy, stamina etc. they need comes from what they eat. To exemplify, the most strong and sturdy health chart of students have been found from the educational institutions where great importance is given to nutritious dietary routine.

Then instead eating home cooked meal, children are more after taste and ready food not realizing the fact how their health is at stake. By educating students about this stuff early on, they will be set up for a lifetime of good habits.

Alternatively, others opine that parents should inculcate good eating habits in children right from their early age because a great part of childhood is spent at home where children learn to relish what they are served with. If a child is fed with nutritious diet, he will develop taste buds for the same and enjoy home cooked meal instead of getting crazy for processed meal packets.

Last not the least, since health is wealth, it is the liability of parents to ensure healthy life for their kids and the same can be achieved by directing them towards good eating habits.

Finally, I would like to stress the importance of educating young generation regarding good eating and both the schools and parents can play their exceptional roles. Schools can include some particular chapters teaching how good eating helps one stay healthy and parents can give them taste buds and thus the wholesome diet will always keep them hale and hearty.

REMEMBER

Summarize the discussion, state your personal
viewpoint, and give a closing thought or implication. It
will help ensure your essay is coherent, logical and ready
to impress the examiners.

100

All cars that burn fossil fuels should be banned and electric cars should replace them. Do you agree or disagree?

The use of fossil fuels powered vehicles around the globe in an advent of nineteenth century which grew more and more and is in high vogue in the present era. Since this phenomenon is proving detrimental to the environment, it is suggested that there should be a strict ban on the use of these auto-mobiles and electric cars should be taken as replacement of them. I firmly believe that switching to electrical cars can be a good alternative.

I raise the argument, keeping in view the damage done by traditional style cars in the past time. Although many efforts are made from time to time, pollution still is on serious hike in mega cities. A thick layer of black dust keeps visibility murky and poisons the air we breathe. All this happens because vehicles emit unpleasant chemicals from their exhausts. Scientific studies over the past few decades have confirmed that these chemicals not only give rise to health issues but are also a major cause of acid rain.

This is in addition to the fact that fossil fuels are limited resources and their extraction from the earth can not only be extremely destructive but the treasure can end too. For all these reasons it is better to discontinue using these vehicles.

On the other hand, relying on electric cars as a substitute seem a wonderful idea as they would be environmental friendly vehicles. Electrical cars mean which run with the power of electricity.
Then generating electricity itself is harmless to nature as only wind, water and the sun sustainable sources are required to generate electrical power. If there are such vehicles which emit no chemicals or gas, the environment will stay uninjured, will effectively reduce carbon dioxide emissions, fight against global warming and contribute to a more sustainable future. There is no exaggeration in saying that electric cars can prove to be the saviors of the planet.

In conclusion, since traditionally powered vehicles are poisoning our echo system, it is a high time to phase out in favour of electric vehicles. Electricity can be generated harmlessly and incessantly and therefore it is better to put a ban on fossil fuel powered vehicles.

Thank You

Dear Esteemed Readers,

I want to convey my heartfelt appreciation to all of you who have embraced my earlier literary works with such affection and zeal. Your steadfast support has been the driving force propelling my ongoing commitment to the art of writing.

The creation of this compilation of essays for the IELTS Writing Module Task - 2 has been a fulfilling journey. I initially embarked on this writing venture with passion, and over time, my enthusiasm for writing only deepened. Each essay in this collection signifies a purposeful and contemplative step forward, much like a performer meticulously choreographing every move on stage.

These essays serve not only as a testament to my dedication but also as valuable resources for IELTS aspirants. My goal is to demystify the writing patterns and recommended sentence structures, illustrating how attainable higher band scores can be. While there isn't a one-size-fits-all technique, the format presented in this collection has proven effective in assisting numerous students in achieving elevated band scores.

Throughout this process, my commitment to honesty in writing has remained unwavering. I firmly believe that the essays, along with the provided writing tips and lexical structures, cater to the diverse needs of IELTS aspirants striving for different band scores. A thorough understanding of these components will undoubtedly contribute to your success in achieving excellent results.

I am optimistic about your journey towards reaching your desired bands and hope that this collection proves to be a valuable asset in your IELTS preparation.
Best wishes for your success!

With sincere gratitude,

AMRITASHAAN

<u>Practice Questions</u>

1. Many employees may work at home with modern technology. Some people claim that it can benefit only the workers, not the employers. Do you agree or disagree?
2. The responsibility to prevent global environmental damage is on politicians rather than individuals. Do you agree or disagree?
3. Some people believe that sport competitions are a source of emotional stress for young people. Therefore, youth should be banned from participating in sport competitions. Do you agree or disagree?
4. Although more and more people read the news on the internet, newspapers will remain the most important source of news for the majority of people. Do you agree or disagree?
5. Many people believe that schools should teach children to become good citizens and workers rather than independent individuals. To what extent do you agree or disagree? Give your own opinion and relevant examples.
6. In some countries, a lot of children have health issues and are becoming overweight. Some people think that the government should be responsible for solving this problem. To what extent do you agree or disagree?
7. In many countries, sports stars earn extremely high salaries. Some people believe that sports stars earn too much money, while others claim that they deserve their high salaries. Discuss both views and give your opinion.
8. Some people think that governments should ban dangerous sports, while others think people should have freedom to do any sports or activity. Discuss both views and give your own opinion.
9. Nowadays, an increasing number of people with health problems are using alternative medicines and treatments instead of visiting their normal doctor. Do you think this is a positive or negative development?
10. Nowadays more tasks at home and work are being performed by robots. Is this a negative or positive development?
11. Global warming is one of the biggest threats humans face in the 21st Century, and sea levels continue to rise at alarming rates.
12. What problems are associated with this, and what are some possible solutions?
13. Due to a more sedentary lifestyle, children in developed nations have higher levels of obesity compared to previous generations. What problems does this cause and what are the possible solutions?
14. In many cities the use of video cameras in public places is being increased in order to reduce crime, but some people believe these measures restrict our individual freedom. Do the benefits of increased security outweigh the drawbacks?
15. Nowadays the way many people interact with each other has changes because of technology. In what way has technology affected the types of relationship people make? Has this become a positive or negative development?

9 7 9 8 8 9 1 3 3 4 9 9 1